MW00564968

MANIFESTING FOR WOMEN

Speed Abundance, Why the Law of Attraction Isn't Working, &
How to Manifest With Divine Feminine Energy

ANGELA GRACE

Ascending Vibrations

CLAIM YOUR *BONUS* MANIFESTING TOOLKIT

Are you DONE with settling for a mediocre life, wasting precious time, & ready to live your wildest fantasies?

• Hack your brain, boost performance, & release blocks holding you back from greatness

• Awaken this amazing energy to supercharge your manifestations

• Stop wasting what little precious time you have on ineffective methods

Manifesting Toolkit Includes:

1. **Supercharged Manifestation EFT Tapping Video** Download To Banish Limiting Beliefs & Propel You Toward Your Dream Life (Infused with 432 Hz Frequency)

2. **Secret Formula Journal** Daily manifestation Ritual Done For You. Simply Rinse & Repeat At Home. (You Can Print This Out, Stick On Your Wall, & Cross Off The Days You Complete The Ritual)

3. **Powerful 10 Minute 'Shifting Your reality' Guided Meditation** MP3 Download (Infused with 528 Hz Frequency)

4. ***BONUS*** LOA boosting 10 Minute 'Feminine Energy Awakening' Guided Meditation MP3 Download

Go Here to Get Your *BONUS* Manifesting Toolkit: **bit.ly/manifestingforwomen**

INTRODUCTION

I am extremely glad that you have landed on this book, dear ladies! Let me welcome you to a sublime world filled with wonders and amazing things ahead. Manifesting is a magnificent tool: as long as you know how to use it. With that in mind, I hope my book gives you not only the inspiration to move forward but also offers you all the information you need to optimize your manifesting performance. In the chapters below, you are going to find step-by-step guidelines about how to perform your manifestations in a way that flows all the positive energy towards you.

Many women are exactly like you—trying to figure out how they can attract all the things they have been craving for into their lives. Even though it might sound easy, you have found the hard way that life is much more than meets the eye. It is most likely that you have already tried to practice manifesting along with other spiritual activities that would bring you closer to your goal. Yet, the results have been much less impressive than what you have anticipated. Why is that? Well, I can tell you right now that by reading through this book, you will identify all these minor setbacks. By doing so, you can rest assured that your manifesting experience will become a lot more exciting and fruitful.

I understand the skepticism as I myself have doubted the power of the universe. I did not realize how my energy affected my reality. Are you doing the same thing: drowning in negative thoughts and expecting something to miraculously take place? You should not get disappointed as true changes cannot happen overnight. They take time and effort. You need to be patient, and allow the universe to work its magic. If you are looking for abundance, then this is what you are going to receive. Let it go, and detach from that persistent thought. This will prevent you from overcharging yourself with unmet expectations. There are no alarm clocks, no time frames, and no deadlines.

Through this book, you will learn a lot about how the Law of Attraction works. Unlike what many people believe, this is not just a gimmick or a trend that has gathered temporary attention until it fades away again. On the contrary, it is a shift in your mindset that is based on a whole philosophical system, and is backed by science. How awesome is that? Two entirely different ways of looking at how things merge and set the foundations of this great tool. Use the Law of Attraction, and you can shape your life in the way you have always wanted. It sounds unbelievable, but I promise you it is the truth.

Starting out without filling the gaps, and truly understanding the meaning of manifesting will not do you any good; in fact, it can even derail you from your initial purpose. Instead, follow the structure that I have included here in my book. Read through the chapters, and keep notes. Organize your mind, and prepare yourself for an extraordinary experience. When you are ready to let that positive energy flow right through you, begin your manifestations. As you see yourself transforming into who you really want to be, as you see the world around you offer you everything you have been dreaming of in the past, you will look back on this moment and be grateful.

Below, you will find my personal journey, as well as a detailed outline of what you are about to read in this book. I hope it helps you fuel your motivation, and inspires you to get that inspirational juice flowing.

MY PERSONAL MANIFESTING JOURNEY

Before we begin this marvelous journey towards manifesting, allow me to share some information about myself. I am experienced in energy healing, Reiki, and crystals. I discovered the power of crystals, energy healing, and spirituality after being introduced to that by my friend, Linda. I am so grateful for her insight and her kindness towards me. This has opened up a whole new world for me, filled with potentials I never even knew existed.

Personally, I have never pictured myself devoted to the spiritual world. In fact, I would even end up mocking those who believed in a higher power. Oh boy, was I wrong! In my life, I have been through various ups and downs; I am guessing most of you can relate to that. No matter how hard I tried, I could not catch a break. After three years of hard work and exhaustion from sleep deprivation, I found myself on the verge of being broke. I felt depressed and unable to enjoy anything in life. What was the point of working so hard if this did not offer me anything in return? I was completely shocked, and honestly, I did not know where to turn to for help.

Linda convinced me to try manifesting. She explained briefly what the Law of Attraction was, and at first I was very skeptical. However, the more she spoke about it, the more it made sense. Maybe this was keeping me away from my goals and dreams. My energy was not aligned to the universe: it felt like a complete revelation. My eyes were wide open, and I literally soaked in every single word she said about energy healing, inner balance, meditation, and everything in between.

I started doing my own research, and gradually reached a point where I could communicate with my spiritual self. In time, I discovered my divine feminine energy, and suddenly my whole world changed. My life transformed—I invited abundance, love, and happiness. No longer did I have to worry about this negativism that spread its shadows over me. I felt better than ever before, and I thank the universe for making that happen.

To this day, I am proud to have written some truly inspirational books that I share with the rest of the world. "Energy Made Easy," "Protect Your Energy," Crystals Made Easy," "Feminine Energy Awakening," and "Reiki Made Easy," are books that have sprung out of my desire to share my journey. I take delight in shedding some light into that knowledge, as I am well aware of the impact it might have on a person's life. Join me in my path, and experience what the universe can do for you!

Are You Ready?

In this book, I am going to discuss what manifesting actually is. Along with the philosophical background, I am also going to help you understand the basics behind the science of vibrational frequencies. Only through this knowledge can you fully grasp the meaning of aligning your energy to that of the universe. Moving on, I will introduce you to several techniques used around the world for increasing your vibrational frequency. Techniques such as EFT, TRE, and hypnosis can contribute greatly to your goal.

Of course, nothing would happen without the divine feminine energy. Therefore, I have dedicated a whole chapter discussing this raw force and how to awaken it from within. The Law of Dharma is another amazing concept, and you will love the seven spiritual laws of success that I have included here. Next, I have focused on love, and how to manifest a loving relationship in your life. You can either set your mind on your ex, or invite a totally new person in your life for a great experience. Later in the book, I will be explaining how certain tools amplify your energy, and maximize the benefits you get out of the process. Visual boards, scripting, positive affirmations, and templates to turn to: these are all elements that will help you structure your manifesting routine.

There are obviously guided meditations available in this book, as well as some hacks to decrease the time frame, in which you can expect your manifesting to come true. I have also referred to some of the most common obstacles that you might encounter throughout your spiritual journey, along with effective ways to overcome those barriers. Finally, I have created a powerful daily ritual that enhances your manifestations. I am sure that you are super excited to read this book. Are you ready to set out on this once-in-a-lifetime adventure?

INTRODUCTION TO
MANIFESTING FOR WOMEN

I guess you have heard about the Law of Attraction at some point in your life. Maybe some of you are skeptical as to whether it is a real thing. Well, to tell you the truth, it is all a matter of physics. The Law of Attraction pretty much resembles the law of gravity. When you let something fall down to the ground from a higher point, then it inevitably falls. There is no question about it since gravity attracts it to the ground: unless you are in space, of course. So, in a similar pattern, your body seems to attract exactly what you have been thinking of.

Let me elaborate a little on that particular process. Your body is filled with energy, vibrating at a pace your mind dictates. You may feel this energy, or you might ignore its presence. In any case, it is omnipresent. So this particular vibration of your body is what attracts certain things to come your way. The biggest challenge is for you to identify how to attract the pleasant things in life. Many people end up attracting everything they have been trying to avoid in the first place. So is this all random?

Luckily, you have control over what you attract. You simply need to figure out how to channel your desires. It all takes place in your mind. Divided into two distinct categories, your conscious and subconscious mind both work their magic nonstop. Ever since you are born, your subconscious gets filled with the stimuli you get. This is where all the memories are formed, along with your habits. In fact, the environment shapes who you are—it shapes your paradigm. All these pieces of information you gather are collected in your subconscious mind, creating who you ultimately become.

On the other hand, your conscious mind is responsible for your thoughts. These are all in alignment with what you receive from the environment. For instance, you see something that makes you sad, and then you think about how to make things right. It is fascinating that, most likely, your thoughts will be in harmony with your subconscious. The two distinct parts of your mind are, in essence, communicating vessels. Your conscious mind thinks in a specific way, which triggers your subconscious mind. Then, your subconscious mind dictates the vibrating energy in your body. Does that make sense to you?

Many people misinterpret the Law of Attraction. They believe it only takes a shift in the way they think in order to benefit from all these amazing things in their lives: if only things were that easy. Nevertheless, it is necessary to dig deeper. If you are really determined to change the course of your life, you need to aim at your subconscious mind. This is where you control your emotions. No matter how hard you try to change your thinking process, the result will stay the same. It goes without even saying that you should try to put aside any hesitation, and step out of your comfort zone. Try to understand what has contributed to forming your emotional mind the way you have so that you can modify it. Be careful, because this is not going to happen overnight. It takes a lot of effort and hard work to achieve something like that. But, at the end of the day, it is all so worth it.

Below, I am going to show you exactly where the problem lies. You might have tried to live by the principles dictated within the Law of Attraction but you have found it hard to do so. However, you need to fully comprehend the basics before you are ready to embark on that wonderful journey: one step at a time. First, we need to understand the science behind the Law of Attraction. Is there really any relevant scientific evidence backing the power of positive thinking? In a nutshell, there is. It all boils down to quantum physics.

UNDERSTANDING THE SCIENCE OF FREQUENCIES

Quantum physics sounds difficult to grasp, right? It might even appear to be intimidating. Yet, understanding the science will unveil the great mysteries of the universe, allowing you to attract the things you want in your life. According to the Hertz Vibration Scale, each emotion reflects a different rate of vibration. Starting at very low frequencies, there are emotions such as shame, anger, guilt, fear, and apathy. As you move up the ladder, you will find emotions like acceptance, love, joy, peace, and enlightenment (Smith, 2018).

This chart indicates that your body's vibration changes, depending on what you feel. Can you imagine that? If you feel guilt all the time, your body's vibration will be low. Therefore, it is inescapable to attract negative things in your life. You cannot help but stay in the same vicious cycle. Or can you? Fortunately, you can change the way you feel. As a result, you will gradually start attracting the proper things that you should experience. Why send out a bad signal in order to receive an identical signal that will only prolong your misery?

Now that you have comprehended the way your body sends and receives signals—resembling radio or TV in a way—it is time to move forward. "How can I use Quantum Physics tools to attract what I really want?"—this is a question that must be popping up in your mind a lot. Well, there are tools that you can use. First and foremost, you need to increase the vibrating frequency you emit. It sounds simple enough, does it not? Unless you understand how you are able to do so, though, it is not going to be consistent. There are many ways allowing you to accomplish that increase in your body's vibrations. The most common of them all include laughter, meditation, and workout.

What you should understand about frequencies is that everything in the universe has one. Nevertheless, there is a special frequency for every little thing in the world that allows that particular thing to perform at its peak. Does that make sense? This is called a resonant frequency and defines the point when something reaches its highest level of oscillation. You understand that everything is vibration: the moment you realize the specific vibration you ought to reach for making the most out of your manifestation, you have what it takes to proceed. With that knowledge in mind, you can never fail in your endeavors.

Another helpful tool is to realize how you feel. Rather than rejecting all the negative emotions, you should first analyze them. Awareness is the first step towards improvement: you cannot have one without the other. Find out the reasons why you are sad, disappointed, or filled with guilt. Rationalize these emotions and then let them go. Aim high at the Hertz Vibration Scale, overflowing with emotions that make you vibrate a lot more. Obviously, you cannot force yourself to love someone. You cannot force yourself to enjoy a specific recreational activity. It should come from within. Hence, what you need to do is figure out what makes your heart skip a beat. What makes you happy is key to attracting happiness. This might sound self-explanatory; however, most people tend to follow a different path in their life, ending up miserable. Find your true colors, and wear them with pride. If there is something your heart is aching to pursue, do not ignore that desire.

It is equally important to surround yourself with people that make you feel good. Their energy is going to lift you up instead of bringing you down all the time. I know that all people come with their special baggage. Sometimes it is their family dragging them down, a toxic relationship, a needy friend. Nevertheless, do you really want to sacrifice your well-being just to avoid confrontation? Are you willing to put your own hopes and dreams on hold purely to continue being poisoned by the toxic presence of those around you? I do not think so! Embrace the people who emit at a high vibrational scale in order to benefit from their positive lifestyle. You will be amazed at the results.

Last but definitely not least, you have to make sure that your mind is set for success. In other words, failure should be eliminated from your dictionary. Failing is not an option. You need to believe in your power and be 100% confident in what you deserve. This is the only way for you to claim what you are entitled to, instead of constantly compromising your desires, your feelings, and your ambitions. It is essential that your mind understands that—your happiness is non-negotiable. Once you realize that deep in your very core, you will feel your vibration elevating. It is pure physics, I am telling you!

Attracting What You Truly Want in Life

Backed by scientific research, the Law of Attraction dictates that positive thinking is essential towards receiving abundance and happiness in life. Ji Young Jung et al have proven that positive thinking has led to increased life satisfaction in life, which is a groundbreaking assumption (Jung et al., 2007). Indeed, it is great to know that your own mind can affect your well-being. There is a strong correlation between the way you feel and the course of your life. If you spend every waking hour complaining and feeling miserable, then you must be sure that your situation is never going to change. Shift your mindset in order to welcome joy in your life. This is science talking, not just me!

If you can dream it, then you can be it. Although it does sound like an advertising motto, the truth is that visualization is deeply rooted to successful outcomes. Where would we be without dreaming, after all? When you want something, you must do everything within your power to achieve that. This means changing the way you feel about yourself, so as to let physics work in your favor. Start emitting high vibration frequencies in order to attract the results that you have been waiting to see in your life. Do not rely on luck or randomness. Do not wait until the stars align and "fate" performs its miracles. Be the master of your own life, and lead it exactly where you want to go.

Let us get back to scientific evidence, which supports the theory behind the Law of Attraction. There are neurological structures, which are called mirror neurons. These structures were primarily found in monkeys, but scientists have interpreted similar ones in the human neurological system. According to the research conducted at the University of Parma, mirror neurons are responsible for beings imitating the behavioral patterns that they observe around them. This means that behavior tends to be imitated, depending on proximity (Jaffe, 2011).

If you are angry, you will most likely notice that those around you imitate that particular behavior. This will happen even if they do not know what has made you angry in the first place. They will sense and pick up on this negative energy, mirroring it to their own self. You will be affected by other people's behavior, of course. In your surroundings, you must have felt that you get influenced by how others feel and they do the same. Mirror neurons contribute to that effect, explaining why this happens to a great extent. We basically exchange energy, becoming aligned to those who are close to us (Jaffe, 2011).

Finally, it is worth considering the fact that intention and action stem from the very same parts of the brain. As a consequence, whenever we stimulate the parts of the brain responsible for what we intend to do, we basically stimulate those parts of the brain that trigger our actions (Gollwitzer & Sheeran, 2006). How does that sound? In this way, it is important to strengthen our visualization of what we want to achieve. Sooner or later, our brain will interpret this visualization as something that needs to be made a reality. There are of course tools that can help you towards enhancing your intentions, basically channeling your desires in a way that enables you to make them come true.

As you can see, there is much more than what meets the eye in the Law of Attraction. Behavior can be interpreted scientifically, offering solid proof that it works. It is worth changing your life by learning the mechanisms that are able to provide for you what you have been dreaming of all this time. Instead of feeling sad that you have not met your goals just yet, get excited about the future ahead of you. This is going to be a bright future, filled with joy and abundance. It is a magical journey that has only just begun. Are you excited to hop on that train, waving farewell to your past insecurity and sorrow?

MANIFESTING YOUR DREAM VERSION OF YOURSELF

The Law of Attraction is absolutely feasible, as long as it starts from within. You must reprogram your mind so as to believe in the new "you" before you are able to manifest it to the world. As you will find out the hard way, the heaviest barrier is placed in front of you by your very own set of beliefs. It is your mindset that has been holding you back, surrounding you with negative energy. Do you really want to remain like that? Do you want to sacrifice your dream version of yourself, simply because you have been accustomed to less?

We should face it: the world is a mirror. The mirror reflects only what you place in front of it. Well, the same happens with your life. If you drown yourself in negative thoughts, fears, and doubts, this is what you are bound to encounter in your life. The same things, over and over again. Unless you do something about it, things will never change. You cannot spend your life waiting for someone else to take charge, and save you from your misery. Why would you do that? You are holding the key to unlock literally anything you have ever dreamed of in life.

It is important to understand that you create the limitations in your daily life, and you are responsible for lifting them altogether.

Otherwise, you will be stuck in a never-ending ordeal. Embrace yourself, and believe that you are worthy of love, wealth, and prosperity. There is a widespread misconception that modesty is the right way to go. As a result, most people tend to avoid praising their inner self. They decrease the value of their accomplishments, and they avoid talking about their strengths: do not fall for that trap. If you diminish your value, others will just think the same. After all, this is what you are going to attract.

Limiting beliefs are the number one culprit preventing you from reaching your dream self. Once you identify them, you need to work hard and eventually eliminate them. Why waste your time self-loathing, when you can conquer greatness? Why would you ever settle for anything less than the life you deserve? It is essential that you realize what the beliefs are in order to fight them off once and for all. You should not let anyone, including yourself, prevent you from walking your special path in life.

Building confidence is of paramount importance here. Allow others to see who you truly are, as the version you have been dreaming of all this time. Stay focused and true to yourself, never missing even the slightest opportunity to shine. I know that at first this will sound opposite to what you have grown up to believe. It has always been the norm to avoid bragging. However, you ought to be aware of your greatness. You need to be 100% confident in your powers in order for others to believe the same. In this way, the Law of Attraction will work in your favor.

In case you are wondering how to achieve that, it takes a lot of time and dedication. There is no more room for self-doubt. No more letting others define who you are. You are a strong, independent individual; you are worthy of love, abundance, success, wealth, and every other thing that you have set your mind on to accomplish. Some great tools that can come in handy for you feature scripting and positive affirmations. Try using a journal, where you clearly write down what you think of yourself. Why are you proud of who you are and what you want to become? Then, use these affirmations in order to cultivate that positive feeling inside you. Nourish your mind with the dream version of yourself, so that you project it to the world and attract it right back.

Obviously, there are several techniques that can help you reach your manifesting goals more efficiently. Among them, you can try out Emotional Freedom Technique (EFT tapping), Trauma Release Exercises (TRE), and self-hypnosis. These tools will enable you to elevate your body's vibration frequencies, getting closer to your target of experiencing the Law of Attraction to its fullest potential.

THE WONDERFUL VIBE OF EFT TAPPING

Have you ever wished you could hack into your brain, boosting your performance? Have you ever wondered if there is a way to optimize your mind's function, modifying what you believe has been holding you back from achieving greatness? I hate to be the bearer of bad news, but the truth is your brain does not come with a detailed manual. If it did, you could study every single page and eventually learn how to tame it. However, there are several techniques out there doing the exact same thing. One of these techniques is EFT, or else tapping. According to EFT, you can change your vibration frequency through gently tapping specific parts of your body. In this way, you can affect your energy and attract equally elevated frequencies in your life (Anthony, 2017).

EFT focuses on the meridian points on your body, therefore resembling acupuncture quite often. While you are tapping the external part of your palm, the third eye on your forehead, your cheeks, or the top of your head, you are encouraged to repeat positive affirmations about yourself. Although at first you might feel awkward doing so, you will immediately experience a boost in your spirit. As you progress with the technique, you will notice that your mental clarity skyrockets. You feel less physical pain and your mood certainly improves.

Below, I am going to guide you through two very simple, yet absolutely brilliant, step-by-step EFT tapping sessions. The first one targets letting go of your limiting beliefs, while the second enables you to attract what it is you have been eager to attract.

Release Limiting Beliefs

It can be hard to deal with your long-lasting beliefs which keep bringing you down instead of lifting you up to where you want to go. It is true that most of us cling on to such beliefs, often sabotaging our course of life. We feel incapable of changing, always returning to the same patterns: it is a slippery slope which we must avoid at all costs. In order to do that, we first need to identify these limiting beliefs. Then, after knowing what we are up against, we will focus on reversing the situation.

First of all, I would like you to close your eyes. Think of a negative, limiting belief. It can be anything, like your conviction that you are not good enough to succeed, or your fear of confronting others. You might see yourself as a lazy person, an individual lacking in educational background, or as a person who does not deserve to be loved. Pick the one thing that causes the biggest discomfort for you. Now, take a deep breath and repeat the following: "I am a lazy person, but I accept that. I love myself despite that." How does that make you feel?

After having done that, start tapping the external part of your palm, saying the exact same thing. Then, move forward with the area in between your eyebrows. Start repeating what you think you are, but this time focus on your actions. Specifically, focus on the actions that contradict your accusation. For example, if you consider yourself lazy, think of all the times when you have proved yourself wrong. All these hard workouts, the times when you had completed a project in time, or the endless days of studying. Continue tapping, this time moving your fingers right next to your eyes. Afterwards, move below the eyes and on your cheekbones.

Tapping is a wonderful way to relax. Tap your chin, and then right above your upper lip. Continue repeating that the specific opinion of yourself is mistaken. Now, start tapping both sides of your chest. You will feel an invigorating sensation slowly overwhelming you. Use positive affirmations, so as to believe deep inside yourself that you do not deserve to be categorized as a lazy person. Tap the area below your arms and then take another deep breath. If you try to repeat your initial belief, you will feel a lot lighter. Try doing the same routine for a week, and you will be amazed at the results.

Attract What You Want

In a similar pattern, you will need to reinforce your belief that what you want actually wants you. This is a very strong feeling, and you should be truly confident to achieve that. First, tap on the external part of your palm with four fingers. Start saying positive affirmations, like the following: "I choose to believe that what I want wants me. I love and cherish myself. Moreover, I respect who I am. I honor myself." Move on to your third eye, repeating the same things: "I love myself, and I know that I am worthy of accepting what I want. It is already on its way, and I have faith in myself."

After the third eye, move below the eyes. Then, tap your upper lip area and your chin. Repeat similar affirmations, which are going to make you feel better: "I know that what I want is available to me. I open myself to receive it." Then, tap your throat and the area below your arm. Once you are done, start over. Start tapping the third eye again, acknowledging that you have been holding back to receiving what you want: "I choose to believe that I have resisted what I want. I am now open to receiving that. I am not holding back any longer."

When you are feeling good enough, start tapping on the top of your head, repeating the following: "I am feeling about the fact that what I want wants me back, and I am ready to receive that in my life." This affirmation is the perfect way to end this session. Enjoy the same session as often as you need to, in order to open yourself up to new possibilities.

Trauma Release Exercises & Self-Hypnosis

Negative energy keeps us at a low frequency. Whatever keeps you at a stressed state prevents you from actually experiencing the benefits deriving from the Law of Attraction. In order to open yourself to the wonderful effects of elevated frequencies, you need to deal with any underlying issues from the past. Face it: the past can be overwhelming. It can be daunting, creeping its way without us even realizing. However, there are ways to settle the score, bury the hatchet, and come to peace with our past traumas. One excellent technique used to release the tension caused by stress is TRE.

TRE stands for Tension and Trauma Release Exercises. It is actually a natural method, which you can see in the animal kingdom if you pay attention to the signs. When you see a dog feeling scared about an imminent threat, you will most likely notice that it starts shaking. Through this repetitive move, the dog releases its tension. Thus, shaking can help restore the balance in frequency within your own body. Your body is more relaxed, vibrating in a positive manner (Emma Claire Donovan, 2019).

You can practice TRE simply by putting pressure on specific muscles on your body. One fine example would be to lean against a wall as you are standing upright, touching the wall with your back. Start slow, opening your legs a little. Act like you are trying to sit down, gently lowering your body and bending your knees. Once you feel your leg muscles burn, hold the position. Gradually, you will notice that your legs are starting to shake. Push as much as you want, without causing discomfort.

Alternatively, you can lie down on your back. Whatever makes you feel more at ease. Bend your knees, so that your feet are touching the ground. Now, try to lift your torso and hips a little. Your legs will start burning, and eventually, you will start shaking. If you feel that the shaking experience is too much, then stop. Stretch and become aware of the process. Repeat the same session over and over again, enjoying the therapeutic release of tension. These soothing tremors will allow you to get rid of the excess energy. In many cases, this is stagnant energy that has been kept into your body all this time.

Once you are fully relaxed, you can turn to self-hypnosis for manifesting your desires. This is another immensely useful tool, which allows you to broaden your horizons. Self-hypnosis is something you can do on your own from the comfort of your own home. Nestled in your shelter, you are free to expand yourself, open up to new experiences, and receive the gifts you have been meant to receive all along in your life. Create a relaxing atmosphere by choosing soft music in the background, scented candles, and a cozy room. Sit comfortably in a chair or on the sofa. Wear something light and look up at the ceiling.

Of course, it goes without even saying that you need to pay attention to the temperature, as well as any other detail that might stand in the way. For instance, if you are feeling extremely hot, you cannot get into a state of hypnosis. The heat will distract you from achieving that nothingness in order to let go of your conscious mind. The same happens if there are constant noises all around you. Make sure that you are able to devote time to hypnosis before moving on with the session.

It is best to do that when you are alone at home or at least when you can have your personal space available to you without any distractions.

Focus on your breathing as you repeat to yourself that you are very tired: you want to sleep. After a few minutes, you will notice your muscles letting go. Breathe in and out slowly, enjoying the silence and absolute harmony all around. As you become familiar with self-hypnosis, you will start adding positive affirmations in this section. You will repeat in your mind the things that you want to achieve in life. What do you want to attract? Picture these things in vivid colors. Be as detailed as you like, concentrating on the conviction that you are on your way to eventually attract all that and more. When you are ready to come back, start counting from one to five. Do not rush it—instead, take your time and become aware of the surroundings.

The first time you practice self-hypnosis might feel a little awkward. After regaining consciousness, you may feel lightheaded. However, you will grow into this experience. After a few sessions, you will require a lot less time to balance between the conscious and the subconscious mind. Moreover, the benefits that you receive from hypnosis amplify as you stick with that pattern. Give it a try, and delve into the mysteries of what lies within you!

❦ 3 ❦

ACHIEVE ANYTHING BY
AWAKENING YOUR DIVINE
FEMININE ENERGY

Are you aware of the divine feminine energy within you? You have been blessed with a powerful force and you may not even know that. In my book *"Feminine Energy Awakening"* I have focused greatly on how every single one of us can awaken that precious energy. This is a life-changing process, which will open your mind to a whole new world. Rather than feeling trapped, unable to release this energy that has been boiling deep inside you, what you need to do is find a way to channel it. Bring it forward, and let it shower you with enlightenment. By doing so, you will see your life fully transformed and shaped exactly the way you have always pictured it to be.

You are a unique being, and you should not be ashamed of your uniqueness. Instead, you should embrace it. Only after having fully comprehended your greatness can you be expected to shine. It is a long process, involving deep soul searching. This is not going to be easy. There are many obstacles ahead, but in my book you will find all the helpful practical guidelines you need. These guidelines will pave the way for you to walk on, discovering your purpose in life. You need to release all the negative energy and become aligned with your own positive feelings. By opening your chakras, you will be able to reach your spiritual self. Through this experience of awakening your divine feminine energy, you will realize that you deserve to be loved and cherished.

This is not a contest of genders,as some might claim. There is no point in comparing the virtues of men or women. It is not a question of who is the best. In fact, there is no reason to get into such a conversation. It will distract you from your deeper purpose, which is to discover your higher self. How can you do that when there are heavy anchors of negative emotions dragging you down? Men and women should not antagonize one another; instead, they should show respect and work together to achieve greatness.

You are special: the sooner you realize that, the better it will be. When you focus on others, you stray from your path towards self-completion. Why would you do that to yourself? Your entity is divine. You are driven by the eternal power of feminine energy which allows you to fulfill your goals. This energy needs to be cherished and nurtured. Do not let others deprive you of that wonderful opportunity to reach new heights. Now is your time to prove your value and expose to the world what you can accomplish.

The divine feminine goddess energy is of exceptional importance, in order for you to reveal your unique personality. If you are determined to embody your timeless greatness, then you should focus on how to awaken that energy. Due to social standards, personal relationships, past traumas, and limitations posed to you by others, your divine energy has remained dormant. However, if you truly want to stand out, and reach out to your higher self, you need to release this power and reap the benefits.

THE ROLE OF DIVINE FEMININE GODDESS ENERGY

One of the key elements in your path to claiming all these wonderful things in life is to be in touch with your feminine energy. Unlike what many people believe, being feminine is not about gender. Take a moment and think about ancient Chinese philosophy. There is the symbol of Yin and Yang, which represents the opposites that coexist in an entity. In order to achieve balance, these opposites are equally important: life cannot be without them (Cartwright, 2018).

In modern society, much attention has been drawn to masculine characteristics. Even women have suppressed their own distinctive traits just because they wanted to fit in. Of course, masculinity can come with its perks. Logic is paramount along with determination, strong will, and fearlessness. However, an individual needs so much more. Where is the emotional wealth, the creativity, and the affection? This is where feminine characteristics come in to save the day. As you can see, every person needs to tread lightly between their feminine and masculine side. This is the only way to accomplish that precious balance in life.

Now, I am sure you have a clear picture in your mind about the way your masculine and feminine energy should work together. How can this be? Well, it is a matter of priorities. When you want to set a goal, you need to bring out the masculine energy of yours. So, before proceeding any further, this is what you should do. Organize everything, setting your goals in a viable plan. Determine the time frame in which you are expected to complete your goals. Stick to the plan, pushing it forward no matter what.

After having done all that, you have created a solid foundation. What is even more important, perhaps, is the ability to receive the good things that you have anticipated through your goal setting. This is time for your feminine energy to step in once more, in order to allow yourself to receive. What is it that you have been eager to get? Is it money, fame, personal growth, love, or affection? Open up your mind and be ready to embrace these amazing things. They might not come to you right away, but they will come. As long as your divine feminine goddess energy is in charge, you have nothing to fear.

Does that sound contradictory to you? Take a look at your business, for example. You have been assigned a very important project.

This project is time sensitive and it relies solely on your performance. If your masculine energy was always in charge, what would you do? You would set your goal to complete a project and then you would constantly push yourself. Do you think this would allow you to finish in time? Chances are that you would feel drained, and exhausted, lacking both energy and creativity. Sooner or later, you would crave for a change.

By taking a break, taking a power nap, or going out for a walk, you would relieve yourself from that constant pressure. After that small pause, your performance would definitely improve. Although continuing on your initial plan might have given you the reassurance that you were doing your best, the truth is far from it. What can you get out of this example? Sometimes, it is best to trust your intuition. There is no point in going to extremes simply because you think you will always cope with the challenges. Harder work is not always the answer. Sometimes, a feminine approach is much more effective in life.

Building trust around you is paramount. Without trust and faith, you cannot succeed in reaching your goals. How can you reach out to love unless you have faith that love is going to come your way? Although your intellect might dictate otherwise, you need to cultivate that trust, and sit still. By doing so, you allow yourself to receive the gift of love. If you kept moving, just like your masculine energy would have suggested, how could you receive love?

Unveiling the Power Within You

Now that you know how important it is for you to discover that hidden source of energy from within, it is time to figure out how to do so. I am sure you feel overwhelmed by the prospect of awakening such a powerful energy, in order to experience your true potential. How can you unravel the mystical force, and let it work its magic? Fortunately, there are many things that you can do. All these small changes in your life will add to becoming more conscious and getting into closer contact with your higher self.

First and forevermore, you should keep a journal. This will track your progress and show you how to move forward. It goes without even saying that it is a long process, and it takes time until you comprehend how your body, mind, and soul become fully aligned.

Through journaling, you can write down every single thing that has helped you in your day; at the same time, you can mention all the little things that have raised a barrier in your efforts. You will use the "trial and error" technique to explore what suits your own personalized needs more.

Then, it is important to heal your inner child. Get rid of all the conflicts, the complexes, and the past traumas: they prevent you from contacting your divine energy. Indisputably, you need to deal with what has happened in the past. If you do not, then you cannot anticipate all the marvelous benefits to be unfolded before your eyes. You must heal the wounds by addressing the issues and resolving them. Of course, this is a strenuous, and often challenging procedure. It needs to be completed, though, before you claim what you are entitled to by birth. How else could you move on with your life?

Positive affirmations will help you come to terms with your divine feminine energy. You can use them as a means to believe in your divinity. Even if at first these affirmations make you feel uncomfortable, you need to step it up, and accept who you are. There is no room for being modest. You are a unique being, and you ought to believe that before reaching the point in your life where you are showered by your divine feminine energy. So, start boosting your self-esteem through numbering your great qualities. You will soon see that you deserve everything.

Along with acknowledging your value, you should also be thankful for what you already have. Count your blessings, and give thanks for the people around you. Be thankful for your health and all the opportunities that have come your way so far. You must realize that life is filled with gifts, and you have already been given a lot. Take a moment to think about it. Maybe you have been blessed with a loving partner or happy children. Perhaps you have skyrocketed your career. Your friends, and acquaintances, and your social network are also people you should be grateful for, unless you feel they are toxic. In that case, it is up to you to remove them from your life.

If you really want to experience absolute calmness, and communicate with your inner energy, try out Reiki and meditation. In this way, you will gradually unveil your defenses. You will look through the glass and see your reflection mirrored without any distortion. Get in contact with your energy centers and your chakras to reveal your power. Enhance your mental clarity, by removing the things that have been clouding your judgment. Find out the truth, and reach the depths of your spirituality. Relax and let go of the worries. Let go of anything that has been troubling you, preventing you from seeing what is out there for you.

You are most welcome to read my book *"Feminine Energy Awakening"* for an in-depth guide on how to awaken this raw force deep inside you. I will be very pleased to help you reach your higher self, embracing your divine nature. It is going to be a spectacular journey towards self-awareness. The world is your oyster, and there is so much you can do. Why should you settle for anything less than what you deserve in life?

❧ 4 ❧
WHY YOU MUST FIND YOUR DHARMA TO BECOME A MAGNET FOR ABUNDANCE

Are you eager to experience ecstasy and exultation in your life? Then you should find your dharma. There is no other way for you to reach genuine prosperity and feel blessed every single day of your life. We are spiritual beings first, after all. Our human manifestation is just a break from our eternal spirituality. First, let us start with an acknowledgment. Everyone has a special purpose in their life: this is the unique gift we have all been given and we are meant to share with the rest of the world.

Each of us has come to this world to discover their true self. Our talents need expression; otherwise, they would just go to waste. However, it is essential that we understand what it means to have a special talent. Think about your life. What are you good at? In fact, what can you say you excel at without thinking twice? Maybe you are great at singing, dancing, building homes, or cooking. Some people are great at creative activities, while others are more practical. No matter what it is that you perform awesome at, you need to stick with it for good.

Now, some might claim that your talent is your way to make money. This is your way to acquire fame and wealth in a materialistic world. Nevertheless, this could not be further from the truth. What you should focus on is helping others. Serving humanity is of paramount importance. This will in turn help you become perfectly aligned with the Law of Dharma. Instead of competing with others, and trying to appear as the best in your field, accept your true calling. Dedicate your life to doing something that will benefit the wider community. Are you a wonderful teacher? Then teach, and allow others to become enlightened through your teachings.

"How can I help the world? What can I offer the world? How can my unique gifts make the world a better, more fun, or more efficient place?" This is not just wishful thinking. Rather than theoretical discussion, this should become the core of your behavior. Rather than trying to overpower others, you need to put them in the spotlight. Your talent and your blessings are there to help. They have been given to you as a vessel to improve the world. Do not ignore this purpose of yours. Fulfill your destiny by bringing joy and happiness to humanity.

Once you get rid of your constant struggle to prevail, you will feel lighter than ever before. As soon as you stop monetizing everything, you will realize that you have been dragging yourself down all this time. Life is not a contest. The world is not filled with enemies— people who you need to stumble on—in order to move up the ladder. There is no point in undermining others, simply to put yourself on a pedestal. You will never reach greatness unless you unveil you prove to be selfless: putting the greater good before anything else.

In modern society, serving others might sound contradictory to what we have been taught ever since we were little. Competitiveness has been advertised as a true virtue, and those who have excelled in a field were seen as leaders. They reaped the fruits of their hard labor, always in comparison with the rest of the world. Still, by doing so, we cannot experience the true meaning of solidarity. We cannot understand how wonderful it feels to help others, without having in the back of our mind the possibility of gaining any benefit out of the process.

As soon as you strip yourself of the burdens that have been weighing you down, you will immediately change your mindset. You will start seeing things in a new perspective, and your entire world will change. No longer being a slave of your own desire and personal gains, you will be free to enjoy life as it really is. This is where the magic starts. The glory of the world unfolds before your eyes, and you start attracting abundance effortlessly. Sounds amazing, right? Try not to waste anymore time. Find your dharma and let life reveal its special purpose for you.

DO SOMETHING TO MANIFEST ABUNDANCE

Some people might think that good things come to those who are blessed. There are people who are lucky enough to receive many blessings in their life, and there really is no point in trying to claim the same on your own. If something comes your way, lucky you. If not, it was surely not meant to be. Well, although I did say that greatness comes effortlessly, this does not mean that you should just sit idle, doing nothing. On the contrary, you must be sure that you are on the right track. The best way to do that is to find your dharma. Comprehend your purpose in life, and concentrate on how to spark joy in another person's life. As simple as that!

What do you do in order to truly reach your deepest thoughts? What is it that drives you towards your higher self? It is essential that you clarify that prior to reassessing your priorities in life. Many people find it helpful to write a journal. Through scripting, you get to identify your weaknesses and reverse any negative situations. When you write something, you immediately make it appear more tangible. In this way, you cannot help but notice that. What you have written is now part of your reality. The scripting process allows you to spot the mistakes in their path, so as to avoid ever making them again. This is a great way to start, but it is not enough.

Meditation is another method used widely so that individuals reach their spiritual presence. You indulge in daily meditation sessions when you get in touch with your inner self. In this way, you calm down your senses, and you reach out to nothingness. This is very important, as it enables you to connect deeply with your source energy. However beneficial meditation can be, it does not work wonders. If you want to relax, it is a great tool to help you get rid of the tension, introducing you to utter calmness. Nevertheless, it takes more than that to attract abundance in your life. As I said before, you need to act. You need to do something, which will allow you to shift your life.

It is not enough to find your unique talent in life. Once you do find what it is, you should not ignore it. Why would you ever want to ignore your talent: your natural inclination in life? You have been given this gift in order to do something. If you just let it go to waste, then you might as well stop trying to improve your life altogether. On the contrary, you should channel your talent in a way that offers something to the rest of the world. If you are a great seamstress, then why not try using that to make amazing clothes for those in need? For those of you who are great at writing, how about you dedicate some time teaching creative writing? There are endless options out there just waiting for you to seize the moment.

When you find your talent, and you let it wither, you do not just cause damage to yourself. This would be self-destructive, but it would only concern you. You would be the one to blame for not following through your ambitions, your hopes, and dreams. However, the truth points out a different aspect as well. You also deprive the world of the opportunity to benefit from this very talent. Rather than contributing to humanity, you choose to sabotage your talent. You do not show others what you are made of, and you settle for less. This results in much fewer possibilities to shine. How can you expect to elevate your spirit and rejoice? A talent is meant to be shared for a greater purpose, so that it enables you to reach divinity.

A talent is a gift not only given to a specific individual, but to humanity as a whole. The world will only be balanced if everyone puts their talent to great use. Therefore, it is your duty to share your talent with the world. It is not up to you to decide, as you are not responsible for acquiring the talent in the first place. As soon as you wrap your mind around that concept, it will become clear what you have been destined to do all along. You will no longer have doubts as to whether you should pursue your dreams, or follow the path your intuition dictates. Just remember, practicing your talent must make you feel happy, satisfied, and complete.

I know that you might be baffled as to what you need to do. You may not know how to behave, in order to succeed in your path towards success. Even if you have the talent, how can you channel it in a meaningful way? What if you are uncertain as to your talent in the first place? Deepak Chopra has analyzed the seven spiritual laws which lead to successful living. These are the vessels which will bring you closer to your divine self. Below, you can read all about these laws that act as guidelines for you to follow. Be sure to structure your life in a way that allows you to respect and love others.

A Glimpse at the Seven Spiritual Laws of Success

In his book, *"The Seven Spiritual Laws of Success,"* Deepak Chopra M.D. reveals how to reach your divinity by finding your timeless spiritual nature. Unlike what you might think, there is no reason for you to strive nonstop, pushing yourself to the limits. When you observe nature, what do you see? A tree grows from a seed, without putting any real effort in the process. It is only natural, so it happens. In a similar pattern, you should let your spirit free, and enjoy watching yourself grow into the divine being you have always been intended to become.

There are seven spiritual laws, guiding you throughout your journey to achieve success. First of all, there is the *Law of Pure Potentiality*. This is a time for you to enjoy silence, ideally meditating once or twice per day. During this time, you sit still and embrace the lack of judgment. The world is filled with potential in their purest form. Moving on, the second law is the *Law of Giving*. This is an exceptional method for making others happy. Give them a gift: it does not have to be something expensive. Just a small gesture of how much you think of others. Even a compliment will do. When others give you a gift, or a compliment, accept with a big smile upon your face. Giving and receiving are two different sides of the very same coin.

The *Law of Karma* is next. Every action in your life generates an equal amount of energy. This energy is directed to you; if you wrong someone or cause pain, then this is going to target you right back. Therefore, you must make sure that you only bring happiness to the world. As a result, you will be showered with love and happiness yourself. Karma is a word often used in modern society, but it rarely has to do with something accurate. It is not a matter of revenge. No matter what it is you think Karma represents, it is just a reflection of the Law of Attraction.

The fourth law is the *Law of Least Effort*. According to that, you need to accept others exactly the way they are. Do not try to change them. Respectively, accept yourself and take responsibility for your actions. If you are constantly draining your own energy, simply to find out that others cling to their behavioral patterns no matter what, this harms you, not them. As soon as you wrap your mind around this, you will see that it is not your place to modify other people's behavior. What you need to focus on is how to accept them. Obviously, you need to accept yourself before accepting anyone else in your life.

The *Law of Intention and Desire* is another wonderful means to reach success. You should acknowledge that every desire comes with its fulfillment. This is an inherent procedure. In case you cannot fulfill a desire, you must understand that there is a reason behind that. Otherwise, you are bound to achieve what you desire in life. The universe will do its best to align, in order for you to get what you want. However, there are things that you should not receive in life. Once the universe picks up on that, it withholds this desire of yours.

Moving on, the sixth law is the *Law of Detachment*. It is important to allow others to be, without forcing them to comply with what you want. Everyone should be free to be whoever they feel like, without any restrictions applied by others. Even if you want someone into your life, you cannot force them. Always remember that life will play out exactly how it was meant to from the beginning of time. Detachment is very important when manifesting. Therefore, you should keep in mind that you cannot spend every moment clinging to your manifestations. You cannot waste your time, always thinking of what you desire. Instead, you need to let go, and watch the magic as it happens.

Last but definitely not least, there is the *Law of Dharma*. As mentioned above, this means discovering your higher self. This is the final destination, leading you exactly where you were meant to be. According to your unique talent in life, you are expected to use it to serve others. This is your deepest purpose in life, allowing you to reach new heights. Do not turn your back to solidarity and unconditional love towards humanity. Your spiritual greatness unfolds through this graceful purpose fulfillment. It is in your hands to discover ways in which you can use your unique talent for good. Remember that it will not only benefit the community, but it will also return to you as a bundle of positive energy (Chopra, 1994).

5

MANIFESTING LOVE

"**A**ll you need is love," at least according to The Beatles and their brilliant song. (Wikipedia Contributors, 2019) Everybody wants to love and feel loved in this world. It is such a wonderful sensation, making you feel warm inside. Along with love comes intimacy, respect, and companionship. Two individuals share their hopes and dreams. They share their fears and find shelter to one another. It is one of the most profound experiences in life. Many people claim that they have been lacking something crucial, until they found their partner. They even refer to that partner as their "better half," or their "significant other."

Each person is free to love whoever truly makes them happy. There are no taboos in love, no hidden agendas, no judgment standing in the way. Such a noble sentiment should not be smeared by negative thoughts or prejudice. Love is meant to take you to the moon, lifting your body and spirit. You no longer walk on the ground: you feel like flying. Who can stand in the way and pass judgment on who you want to share this splendid feeling with? It is a pure form of art, and there are no boundaries in art.

Love is a powerful driving force, motivating people to reach their greatness. People tend to become better once they have found someone who loves them. They put aside their selfishness, and they do things to benefit another human being. In other words, they serve humanity. Is that not what dharma is all about? As a result, they find a new purpose in their life, and it makes them better people. Even though they had been living on their own all this time, now they have discovered a new way of seeing things.

However, love is not so easy to experience. There are many people who have never found somebody to make them feel this way. At the same time, there are those who have never been loved...at least, not in the way they had been looking forward to being loved. Eluding love throughout your life seems extremely saddening. But, how can it be? Why is it that not everyone finds their perfect match? Is it really that difficult to run into the love of your life?

Ever since we are little, we get used to anticipating Prince Charming: he is going to come to our rescue. However, why would we want to let another person take charge of our life in the first place? There is no point in feeling helpless. Love does not have to be like that *"quid pro quo."* You should love someone because you want to, not because you have to do so. It is important to realize that you can survive without love. You are the one who will change your life and shape it exactly the way you have always wanted. Love will set you free and allow you to reach new heights. This is not a matter of survival; instead, it is the pursuit of happiness that defines one's need to love.

After having clarified that, it is necessary to appreciate the meaning of love manifestation. If you want to attract who you are going to love, you ought to figure out how to do so. Why waste your time surrounded by people who you do not find appealing? Why spend countless hours feeling sorry for yourself? Rather than settling for a loveless life, you need to take matters into your own hands, and call out love's name. You have the key to unlock the door and experience what you have been craving for your whole life. No one else is responsible to do that but you.

By manifesting love, you will have the opportunity to attract the feelings that you want others to show you. Remember all these endless nights when you have been visualizing the partner of your dreams? Now time has come to reincarnate those dreams. Instill life into your fantasies, and reach out to what you want to taste. The sweet agony of love, the memories that stay imprinted within your mind, the adrenaline spike, and the magic moments you spend together. Your heart skips a beat, and you feel like you have found your soulmate. Sounds breathtaking, right?

ATTRACT YOUR PERFECT MATE

Become a love magnet, and attract the partner of your dreams. In order to do so, you must project love. Otherwise, how can you receive it? It is a matter of balancing the energies. If you remain idle, avoiding to feel genuine emotions, and constantly struggling to build fences, then this is exactly what you are going to get in return.

One of the best ways for you to attract love is through EFT tapping. I have shown you earlier in the book how to change your body's vibration frequencies through this powerful technique. In this case, I am going to focus on the method of magnetizing the person you want, inviting them into your life. You can do that by indulging in a simple, yet very effective session. What you need to do is relax, and dedicate some time to tap specific meridian points of your body while at the same time repeating romantic affirmations. This will not only elevate the energy you are emitting, but it will also allow you to calm down your senses, and focus on what is important.

Try to get rid of any distractions. After all, you should dedicate these moments towards visualizing what you want to achieve, when it comes to feelings. "Why do you want to attract love?", "Are you worthy of being worshiped?", "What makes you a great person for someone to fall in love with?"; these are some of the questions you need to answer through this tapping experience. You must clarify all these issues before being able to move forward with attracting your dream partner.

Start slow by convincing yourself of what you should already know. "I love myself, and I honor myself. I am worthy of being loved, and I deserve to love someone deeply" is your opening line. This sets the tone of what comes next, which is none other than your love claims. You are an independent, powerful being that longs for sincere affection. You are not willing to settle for anything short of that, which should be non-negotiable. Since you have set the bar so high, it is only fair that you maintain absolute focus throughout the process.

Whatever insecurities you may have, now is the right time to encounter them. Change the way you feel about your alleged "flaws" through pointing out how invalid they are. For example, have you spent your whole life thinking that you are ugly and undeserving of love? This is what has dragged you down, preventing you from experiencing the true wonder of affection: you should change this conviction. Take a look at yourself. What is it that makes you smile? When you do smile, do you notice your eyes shining? It is true: you are beautiful. Add that to your affirmation.

Starting from the external part of your palms, as always, you must continue tapping at the face. The third eye area, right between your eyebrows, beneath your eyes, on your cheekbones, and above and below your mouth: these are all excellent parts stimulating energy. Then, move down a little. Tap your throat, which is where another important energy center is located. This is crucial for communicating your thoughts and your emotions. Next, you should tap above your chest, and reach your heart. Gently tap there, and feel your body aligning to your heartbeat. It is your circadian rhythm, so enjoy this perfect balance you have achieved.

End your EFT tapping session with a deep breath. I am sure you are feeling better, having boosted your confidence. Moreover, you must have increased your focus on what you need to pursue in life. Love is not something distant, and it is hardly out of your reach. However, you should reach out your hand and touch it. Even after having found love, you need to be delicate, and always strive to make your relationship stronger. There is no other secret to a healthy relationship other than brutal honesty, unconditional respect, and hard work.

Commitment in the Relationship

I am sure you are going to reach your goal and get the partner of your dreams, as long as you follow the guidelines that I have shared with you in this book. Nevertheless, this is just the beginning. First of all, allow me to congratulate you on having manifested the right person in your life. Now you need to become accustomed to the idea that this person is going to stay right by your side for as long as you want. There is no reason why you should not embrace the whole "till death do us part" thing, assuming that you like that idea. But, we should face it: there are still several bumps along the way threatening to destroy what you have already accomplished.

Keeping a relationship is just as hard as attracting it in the first place. You need to make sure that the relationship is always thriving through an ongoing process of evaluation. As you go, you need to check the status, and report any negative glitches. In this way, you can assess, and remedy everything ahead of time. I know this is easier said than done. Still, you must pay attention. Some people tend to let go, and settle for the fact that they have found a special individual in their life. They stop trying, which means they give up and never do anything to improve themselves.

If you are determined to maintain a viable relationship for the long run, then you must remember to water the flower of your love. This is the only way for you to ensure that it remains thoroughly flourished, and never dries out due to lack of care. I know you will be expected to do more than what you might have been used to, but it is definitely worth it. Since you have chosen a specific person to be your partner, you need to show respect and deep understanding. Do not just harvest the fruit of your labor. A relationship is a living and breathing organism. Unless it is nurtured, it is going to die out sooner or later.

Although each relationship has its ups and downs, one thing is for sure. You should keep the fire burning in order to maintain your initial passion. Remember what has drawn you to that person and what has made you fall in love with them. Why have you gone to extremes to conquer their heart? It is the same person standing before your eyes, asking to be loved eternally. Why have you stopped trying? There is nothing worse than indifference. I am sure you would hate it, drowning in a relationship that stagnates. Do not contribute to decay when you can instead breath fresh air to it.

Let your inspiration lead the way. Surprise your significant other, letting them know that you still care. It does not have to be something big. Just a flower or a morning note neatly placed by the bedside table. A text message you send on your way to work, expressing your true emotions. How about you get out of your comfort zone for a while? Even if you do not know how to cook, give it a try. Prepare a special dinner just for the two of you. Your partner is going to love that gesture. Even if the result is not up to par, it will mean something truly wonderful for your relationship. Then, celebrate your milestones. An anniversary is somewhat the norm, but try to figure out other things in your common path that have stood out among the rest. The first time you went on a vacation overseas, or the day you moved in together. These are small victories you should cherish for a lifetime.

Prepare yourself for some losing battles. Even if they seem that way, they allow both of you to let some steam off and move on with the good things about your relationship that have kept you going all this time. Compromising is not such a bad strategy by default, especially when the prize is your happiness. I am not saying that you should oppress your feelings, or give in to impossible demands. No, of course not. If that happens, then you have attracted the right person in your life. Reassess your priorities, think of what you actually want, and project that to the world.

Last but definitely not least, find the right balance between doing things together and allowing some space for your partner to breathe. It seems tricky, but you will get there. Just think of it as an opportunity to catch up with your friends, read, take on a new hobby, or just chill. There is no point in spending every single moment together with your partner: you will both feel suffocated in the end. Why subject your relationship to this ordeal? Instead, make every moment you spend together count. Do things that you will be looking forward to throughout the week. Your experience should be fun!

Now that you have cleared the air as to how to manifest love, how about attracting a specific person in your life? I am sure you have already set your mind on someone or you are pretty close to finding the ONE. What happens next?

✣ 6 ✣

MANIFESTING A SPECIFIC
PERSON

I t is amazing to acknowledge that you are ready to love and be loved back. This shows that you have matured in life and you want to share your emotional treasures with someone special. But, who is this person? We are often open to meeting new people, inviting them into our lives, and evaluating our relationship as we go. However, there are times when we have already decided about who we would like to see in our life. Even though at first this might sound very restrictive, in time you will realize that it is a true blessing in disguise. Not only do we know how we want to feel, but we are also certain about who we want to feel it with. How awesome is that?

There are moments in life when the universe seems to be fully aligned with your desires. In these moments, you feel like the luckiest person alive. Falling in love definitely ranks high in that list. Especially when your love interest shows exactly the same emotions, you are over the moon! How could you not be? I am well aware of how intoxicating love can be, overwhelming you with that warm sensation that lets you know you have found your perfect match. Yet, not everyone gets to be that lucky. Unfortunately, on several occasions you will encounter people who have never found their match; on the contrary, there are those who have found them, but they have been left craving for a relationship.

I know what you are about to say. You cannot force somebody to have feelings for you...or can you? Let me rephrase that for you, in order to reflect reality. Instead of worrying about forcing another person to have feelings for you, how about you admit that they would be lucky to have you in their life? You are not a random person, are you? In that sense, you are doing them a favor. You are opening their eyes, attracting them into a life filled with light, happiness, and abundance. This should be your mentality, prior to engaging in a sensational love hunt.

The most important thing to remember is that your body's vibration frequency needs to be balanced with theirs. In order to do that, you must be extremely careful. No negative thoughts should flood your mind, as they will most likely lead to a low frequency. Unless you wish to settle for a life in misery, and disappointment, avoid such thoughts for good. You need to open yourself to positive emotions, gradually building your momentum. What a better way to achieve that than through a wonderful visualization? Allow me to show you how to invite this special someone into your life. Of course, you can indulge in this session even when you do not have a specific person in mind.

Visualize the person you want to see in your life, and picture every little detail. The color of their hair, the sparkle in their eyes, the small lines on their face, the shape of their body, the way they dress, and the way they make their hair. These are all special touches which have led you to love them so dearly in the first place. Hence, they deserve to be mentioned, and you need to focus on these special attributes of your love interest. Once you have painted their picture in your mind, you are ready to move forward to the next step. Feel them moving towards you, getting closer and closer with every breath you take.

As soon as your dream partner has reached right before your eyes, and you can feel their breath warming your lips, you can concentrate on their movements. Feel their hands slowly touching your palms, arms, and shoulders. They are moving upwards, and then they are touching your neck, and finally your face. Feel their fingers fondling your cheeks and then touching your hair. They are smiling at you, and they are whispering in your ears. I am sure this gives you goosebumps, and you are already experiencing that exciting sensation.

Now, remember that you must combine this visualization along with several positive personal affirmations. In this way, you will optimize the effect of this session on your mindset, and eventually on the energy you emit. Below, I have prepared some of my favorite affirmations to share with you:

- I love myself deeply and unconditionally.
- I am worthy of being loved.
- My chosen partner and I share deep, true feelings of love and devotion.
- I am happy to have my significant other into my life.
- My chosen partner is 100% committed to our relationship.
- Our relationship is true, meaningful, and honest.
- We are both happy to be in this relationship that will last for a lifetime.
- My significant other respects me totally and honors my personality.
- I am grateful for all the love I receive in this world.
- I am thankful about all the blessings I have in life.
- My chosen partner is deeply in love with me, and the feeling is mutual.
- I am sure that our relationship is going to last forever.
- There is nothing that can separate me from my significant other.
- I have been blessed with love; I have been showered with love.
- My chosen partner and I are a wonderful couple.
- My significant other and I are meant to be together.
- I am so happy to have such a loving, caring partner in my life.
- I have no doubt that me and my partner belong together.
- My chosen partner always tells me how beautiful and intelligent I am.

- I have a deep spiritual, physical, and emotional connection with my partner.

By repeating those affirmations, you will strengthen your self-confidence. In this way, you will project it to the world, attracting what you deserve. The specific person you have set your mind on will have no other option, but to fall into your arms. This will happen sooner or later, there is no need for you to worry about that. Just embrace your destiny, prepare for what is about to take place, and wait for the magic to unfold before your eyes.

HOW TO GET YOUR EX BACK

Dealing with an ex can be really heartbreaking, I am well aware of that. I am sure there are deep wounds that never seem to heal, no matter how far you have moved on in your life. There is always a person who has scarred you, and this scar has become part of who you are. In case your ex is a toxic person, I am going to insist on letting go and seeking a new partner. Although you may feel hooked on this individual, you should know that you need to pursue light in your life; avoid the darkness and all the toxicity that lurks in the shadows. It will drag you down, drain you of your energy, and leave you exhausted, disappointed, and helpless. Is this the life you have been dreaming of throughout this manifesting process?

Let us assume that your ex is not toxic. Take a moment and concentrate on what has driven you away from each other. Was it an act of infidelity? If this is the case, then what will stop your partner from doing the same thing again in the future? Maybe you have just drifted apart due to lack of common interests. Distance can get in the way and mess with relationships. Not many people can handle endless miles separating them day-by-day. Perhaps that flame has burned out eventually, leaving you reminiscing those times when you could not get enough of each other.

No matter what the special circumstances have been that lead to your breakup, you need to do some serious soul searching. What you need to figure out is if you truly want to have your ex coming back to you. Do you honestly want to get your ex back, or is it just a whim? You do not care to admit it, but your separation might have caused you the repulsed desire to get your partner back in your life. On some occasions, people tend to forget about the bad things. They focus on the wonderful memories that they share with their ex, often idolizing them. So, take a deep breath: ask yourself if this is really what you want to achieve through manifesting.

Even after having concluded that you want to try again with your ex, you still have to come to terms with a disturbing fact. No matter what has happened between you two, you were the one to blame. Of course, this does not mean that you should beat yourself up or assume full responsibility. It is important, however, that you know where to look, and connect the dots. When the relationship collapsed, you may have tried hard to understand why. Perhaps you confronted your ex in order to find out the truth. Yet, you need to realize what has been the driving force that resulted in pure havoc. What has led to your relationship collapsing right before your very eyes? Is it still a mystery to you?

I know that it has been a while since you two were a couple. Nevertheless, it would be great if you could recall some memories you have of the time period prior to your breakup. If you look more closely, you will start noticing a pattern. You had started questioning your partner's feelings. In fact, you had begun thinking that you were not enough. You had lived in fear of abandonment, practically waiting for your partner to break up with you. Maybe you had read the signs wrong, or maybe there was a slight sliver of evidence backing your fears. Either way, your thoughts had been piling up for so long, creating low body's vibration frequencies.

As a consequence, you basically attracted the breakup. You made sure that your partner started seeing these signs, feeling them deep inside, and eventually leaving you. Does that sound familiar? Is this the way you behaved before you broke up with your ex? I am pretty sure about the answer, as this is how quantum physics works. You think about something intensely, ignoring anything else. Over time, your thoughts become the reality. You project them to the world and end up attracting the very same thing. You have been looking forward to using this specific mechanism in your favor, manifesting love, wealth, and happiness.

Every experience can turn into a lesson for you, allowing you to become wiser as time passes by. Never again should you project these negative thoughts to the universe, as they are bound to come back and sabotage your life. You do not need to worry about a potential breakup. If you do break up, then this is what you were always meant to do in your journey towards reaching your higher self. *"Que sera, sera"*, or else *"Whatever will be, will be."* (*Que sera*, 2019) No one knows what the future holds for them, but you should have faith in your divine spirit.

Assuming that you still want to get your ex back, you need to start projecting that to the world. Begin visualizing that you already have your ex in your life. Close your eyes, and think of your partner's presence beside you. They are standing right in front of you, almost touching you. Take a moment and observe every single detail about their physical appearance, as well as their posture. Are they showing any affection towards you? I bet they are. It is prudent to enhance this visualization with some positive affirmations. Feel their arms around you, and their breath as they are whispering sweet nothings. Imagine that you are already together, just like I have shown you above, targeting a specific person.

Repeat the same ritual as often as you like, always maintaining the same positive attitude. Your ex will be drawn to you sooner or later, enabling you to enjoy your relationship with them. Do not be pessimistic: believe deep in your soul that you are together. This is the first and most important step to take in order for this dream of yours to come true. Just remember that some things work out exactly the way they are supposed to, even if we do not want to admit that. That being said, set out on this wonderful adventure and pursue your fantasies!

A Common Mistake to Avoid Like the Plague

You have mastered the art of manifesting a specific person, and you are ready to put theory into practice. Are you starting to feel excited? Be careful, though, as you may fall for the oldest trick in the book and sabotage your own endeavor. Have you ever felt like nothing ever works out the way you have expected it to, despite your hard labor? Well, there is a reason why this happens. Although you have planned out every single detail, it seems that you have neglected the importance of a little thing. It is a pity to let that stand in the way, and prevent you from reaching your "happy ending."

Let us get more specific about the single worst scenario that can play out when manifesting love. You focus on the way your partner is going to be. While doing so, you concentrate on their physical appearance, and then you outline the features you want them to have. A kind and gentle partner, witty, understanding, with a great sense of humor, and wealth: seems like a keeper, right? Next, you manifest the feelings you expect of this partner. This specific person must be madly in love with you, showering you with affection. What a better way to boost your self-confidence than a constant reminder that you are unique?

I am sure you are reading these lines with a huge smile on your face. I do not blame you: this is what we all want in life! It is so invigorating to experience love in its purest form, making you feel like a million dollars. Nevertheless, what about the other way around? Have you ever thought about that? It is awesome to find a person who truly loves. A person who will go above and beyond just to be with you. It is what we all dream, a partner who will be utterly devoted to us no matter what. This is what most of us have grown up to wish for, when we lay in bed at night. Still, how about our feelings towards them? Do they not matter as well?

The huge mistake that you are about to make is not to pay attention to the way you feel towards your manifested love interest. How will you feel towards your special person? Unless you manifest that too, you risk ending up with an unfulfilled romance. This means that you will enjoy the love, and affection of the person you have attracted in your life. However, your feelings will not be mutual. You will not be madly in love with your dream partner, and this will spoil your long anticipated emotional equilibrium. In the end, you will feel like you are to blame for all this mess. After all, the relationship is never going to last, if you do not share the same enthusiasm. Sooner or later, it will crumble into dust.

Do not get me wrong: it is perfectly understandable to love yourself, and make sure that you attract someone who loves you the way you deserve to be loved. You should continue pursuing happiness and sparking the feelings you are entitled to in life. At the same time, though, you must make room for manifesting how you want to feel towards your dream partner. It goes without even saying that you should aim at a balanced relationship, meaning you feel pretty much what your significant other feels. Otherwise, your chances of staying together for a long time decrease dramatically.

In a nutshell, the big drawback you need to steer clear from is the lack of focus on who the partner is going to be and how you are feeling about the specific individual. If you are determined to embody the experience of mutual, intense love, you need to be careful throughout your manifestation. Whether you are thinking of a specific person who already exists in your life, or you are manifesting a totally new individual, you must pay attention to your feelings towards them. Incorporate how you are going to feel, so you avoid the realization that you are just not that into the person you have invited in your life, because let me tell you, this is going to be a hot mess!

THE POWERFUL
MANIFESTING TECHNIQUES

T here are so many wonderful things just waiting ahead in your life, I can promise you that. The thing is that every single person has different desires, different needs, and different wants. How can you manifest these things into your life? This book aims at giving you all the necessary tools which will allow you to welcome anything you have been dreaming of into your life. Manifestation is real and it is out there. It is now in your hand to reach out and grab exactly what you like.

In this chapter, I am going to focus on journaling and scripting. These are the two sides of the same coin, meant to serve as your lucky charm. I know some of you might be skeptical as to why you need to devote time and write down what you want to achieve in your life. *"Isn't visualization enough?"* you may argue. Writing is a cathartic activity, which can help you cleanse out your body from within, just like a detoxification diet would. Even though you are having doubts, let me reassure you that you are going to love it.

First of all, you need to create a lovely atmosphere. You must be looking forward to your scripting time. This should not be a boring, tedious concept. It should not be something you only do because you have to. If you consider journaling a mere obligation, then it is only going to backfire. You will never receive what you are writing about, which will definitely lead to more doubts on your behalf. This is a vicious cycle that benefits no one. I would strongly advise you to give it a chance, and dive right into scripting with a positive attitude.

Find a journal that truly makes your heart beat faster. It needs to be something you enjoy writing in. You do not have to go overboard when it comes to the actual cost of the journal. Just pick something that appeals to you a lot. Maybe add some color, or find a luxurious treat that you can resort to for manifesting your dreams. Alternatively, you can also write letters on a piece of paper. Literally the sky's the limit, and you can experiment with scented paper, fancy pens, and pencils. Of course, you can always resort to the digital form of journaling. Yet, nothing beats the sensation of writing on a piece of paper. You watch letters transformed into words, and this is something you made from scratch. It is such a creative activity.

There is no right or wrong as to where you should write. Some people sit on their desk, whereas others prefer to be fully relaxed, so they choose their bed or a comfortable sofa. Just do whatever makes your boat float, because you need to feel good about the entire process; otherwise, you will not stick to this habit for long. Create a cozy ambiance, maybe put on some lounge music that relaxes you. Light a scented candle with a lovely aromatic character, and sip on your favorite herbal tea. Get those creative juices flowing. This is your moment, so relish it.

Now that you know how to write, it is equally important to clarify what you should write about in your journal. Some people think that they should write everything they have ever wished for, exactly like they did back in the day with their letters to Santa Claus. As a result, they end up completing a list of things they want to attract in their life, and then they expect for every wish to come true just like that. However, scripting does not work in this way. This can only work when you are a child, provided that your parents take a moment and read through your list. Then, you can expect to find a great surprise under the Christmas tree.

Start slow, and be consistent. Do not just try out scripting when you have nothing better to do. Instead, you should make sure to indulge in this relaxing activity on a daily basis. This will allow you to become fully conscious of the things you want to attract in your life. When you begin this creative habit, you will soon find yourself drawn by your emotions. An inner drive will guide your actions, and enable you to fill whole pages with your thoughts, your projections, your intentions, and positive affirmations.

SCRIPTING AS A GREAT LAW OF ATTRACTION FORCE

Scripting will most likely change your life, as long as you let it. In order to do so, you need to decode its purpose. When you are journaling, you are writing about the things that you want to draw into your life. This is the very core of the Law of Attraction, after all. Vibration attracts vibration. First of all, you should be very excited about the things that you write. Do not just go through the motions, without adding emotion into the mix. If you avoid feeling when you write, then you might as well stop right now.

Besides, look at it this way. When are you used to acting, rather than contemplating? I am sure feelings are involved in your actions. They grow, and flood you with an energy that wants to burst out of your body. This is when you act and release that energy. Do not just write indifferently. Make every word count. If you are not in the mood, do something else. You can always write when you feel like it. In this way, your vibration will skyrocket, and you can attract the things you write about effortlessly. If you are emotionally involved, I guarantee that your manifestation will become a lot more intense.

That being said, there is a widespread misconception that you had better steer clear from when scripting. You might get overly enthusiastic, and wish for things that are never going to happen. For example, you cannot project to the universe your desire to get a lot tallert. This can never happen, no matter how hard you try. In other words, you should believe in what you are scripting, setting fairly realistic goals that you can achieve. Do not get me wrong: you can always dream big, but you need to include things that you believe can happen in scripting. In a different situation, your subconscious brain decodes your desire as false, and does nothing to proceed with its realization.

When you write in your journal, remember to be precise. You need to have mental clarity, and include details about what you want to achieve. If you only mention your goal, then how can you expect it to be realized within a specific time period? In avoidance of any distortion of your desire, leave no room for speculation. Do not be vague; instead, add as many little things as you can into your description. Some people might be afraid of offering too much information. This could backfire, since it would limit their options, right? I do not know if you share this opinion, but the Law of Attraction does not work like that.

I am telling you again, do not shy away from details. For instance, when you are manifesting a specific person, you should include their physical appearance. Along with that, you should add the personality traits that you love about them, as much as those that you want to avoid. Finally, you need to be accurate in your time frame. When did you meet this person and where? What do you both feel? All these details will help you accomplish your goals exactly in the way you want. Otherwise, it will be pretty much like you are gambling. Obviously, it is possible that you do not have your mind set on a particular person. You do not need to, as long as you describe the specific characteristics you have been searching for in that person.

A lot of people tend to be indecisive in their scripting experiences. They start manifesting one idea, and after a few days they move onto the next. It is a rollercoaster of emotions, as one manifestation is constantly swiped with another one. This can result in pure havoc and chaos. You are looking for balance, not chaotic situations. When you do not follow through with your description, you cannot make it happen. If you are afraid of making a decision, then you should not write about anything in life. In fact, you should not engage in the Law of Attraction. But, is it not the main purpose of reading this book? Make a decision, and wear it with pride. Commit to your decision and enjoy it as it becomes reality.

One word of caution before moving forward with an outline of what to include in your scripting: do not fall for the *"wishful writing"* trap. As mentioned before, you should have the attitude of already witnessing the benefits of your accomplishments in life. Do not write as if you are wishing for something to become true. This would confuse the universe, and it would certainly create a different vibration for you. It is already true, and you are experiencing its wonders to the fullest. You are projecting how you feel, after accomplishing that particular thing, and keeping it into your life. As a result, you attract the very same emotions. As simple as that!

A Template That Makes Scripting a Piece of Cake

There really is no "one-size-fits-all" approach in scripting. You basically start writing in your journal, and you watch the magic happen. In fact, before you know it, you will see your thoughts transformed into words. They will literally flow from your mind and fill the blank sheets of paper with your most wonderful wishes for the future. It is purely great to channel these dreams and fantasies of yours into something creative. After a while, you can turn to these journals and read all about them. This is a way to keep track of your progress, evaluating how much you have actually managed to manifest into your life. Pen and paper is all you need in order to form the foundations for reaching your goals. Indulge in freewriting, so as to let your thoughts lead the way.

Confidence building scripting is a great way to boost your ego and truly appreciate yourself. Even if at first you will feel slightly uncomfortable, you do need to adhere to the routine of praising yourself for everything you have accomplished so far. This is not a race, so it does not matter how much time it takes you to achieve your milestones. The only thing that matters is that you move towards the right direction. A technique used to build confidence, and project what you want to attract, is through writing letters.

In case you want to write a letter of gratitude, a thank you letter, or a note that explains what you have succeeded in doing, I have prepared a practical template to use. In this way, you no longer have to worry about what to write. Just follow the guidelines below, copy, and add to your manifesting routine. It is best that you complete writing the letter, and then keep it somewhere within your reach. Read it out loud, so that you get to believe every single word you are saying. You can keep it by your bedside table, and read it when you wake up, and again when you go to sleep. Do so for 20 to 30 days, and then store it somewhere neatly. When you come across that letter after some time, you will be greatly surprised!

Thank you, _____ (This is where you insert the name this letter is addressed to. It can be what you believe in, a guardian angel, a spirit, a mythical presence, a person you look up to, an influencer, or a specific person in your life.)

I am truly grateful for everything I have in my life. It is great to have such health, happiness, love, and abundance showering my existence. (In this section, you start by giving thanks for all the good things that have happened in your life and all these things that you want to achieve. In that way, you mention as if you were already experiencing them.)

I have achieved my personal, and professional goals _____ (This is the time to be specific, so write down everything you want to have in your life: both as a person and as a professional.)

I now have _____ I have been enjoying love, and happiness every single day.

Thank you, thank you, thank you so much _____ (Repeat the name you have addressed this letter to.)

As you can see, this is a quite simple, yet effective outline for a gratitude letter. You can always add your personal touches, of course. By all means, be creative. Still, do not be modest, or shy away from claiming what you want to achieve. Be firm and positive. Write like you are already reaping the fruit of your manifestation. Activate the feeling of already having these things in your life. Then allow yourself to forget what you have written. Move on: concentrate on other things. Clear your thoughts, be creative, and live your life. Last but not least, be pleasantly surprised as these things come into your life.

Use this template to create a gratitude letter directed to your parents, or the people who have inspired you in your journey so far. Make sure to write thank you letters, big or small, to those who have contributed to who you are. Apart from that, do not forget to write down letters including gratitude to people who you would want to have in your life. Write as if they have already helped you and you want to give thanks to them. In this way, you cultivate the feeling of gratitude on various levels. You enhance the feelings you have experienced in life, and at the same time, you are projecting the emotions you want to experience.

❧ 8 ☙

MANIFESTING YOUR DESIRE
IN 30 DAYS

Do you want your desire to come into fruition? Very well. How much time can you invest in accomplishing that goal? Time is money, and you should not let it go to waste. Instead, you need to make every minute count towards your self-accomplishment. Luckily for you, there is no rule stating that you should spend an enormous amount of time preparing for the Law of Attraction. It is all about you coming into alignment with what you want. Once you find that precious balance, the world is your oyster.

Strengthen what you believe of yourself. This is one of the primary goals you should set. Journal every day and describe whatever you do. In this way, you will be able to understand where you are blocking your success. On the other hand, journaling will also enable you to identify all the situations where you have showered yourself with positive energy. The things that are showing up in your life derive from your vibrations. Unless you realize that, you can never expect to reach these goals of yours.

Believe in your inner power, as it is indisputable. Positive affirmations will help you in your effort to grasp your power. Get in the frequency of your desire. Believe that you are worthy of amazing things in life. You should not let anyone tell you differently. You are great, and this is non-negotiable. What makes you unique, though? Think about that and write down as your thoughts become reality. What you must make sure of is that you project that confidence to the world. This will in turn open up a whole new world of opportunities, because this is what you will draw closer to you.

If you are determined to succeed, then it is essential that you share your initial enthusiasm about the whole process of manifesting. Why did you look this philosophy up in the first place? I am sure that you have read somewhere about this wonderful secret that makes your mindset shift. From your experience in life, this is exactly what has been dragging you down, so you thought you would give it a try. A few minutes later, you were blown away by the innumerable possibilities unfolded before your eyes.

What has changed since your first reaction? The Law of Attraction is a powerful gift, so why would you ever get disappointed? If you are seeing no tangible results, maybe you should reevaluate your strategies. Assuming you want to speed up the process, there are a lot of things that you can do. Powerful manifestations that I am describing below will allow you to achieve what you want in a fraction of the time it would normally require for your manifestation to complete. Take charge of your life, and start working towards making things happen.

Do the things that make you feel better. In this way, you will lift your spirit and ensure that your body's vibration frequency becomes radically elevated. Make the Law of Attraction fun again. Avoid suppressing your desires, and succumbing to what society dictates. Now it is your time to shine. Enjoy the ride, and do not settle for any other substitute. Get inspired, since it is the inspiration that drives your spirit to greatness. Be mindful of the experience, and appreciate the moment. This is what being in the present means, after all.

Finally, I would have to insist on stating what you want. Of course, scripting is a wonderful way to manifest your desires. However, you should never underestimate the power of expressing those desires verbally. You can do it out loud, or you can simply whisper these projections. Do not worry—the universe is always listening. The fact that you say all the things that you want to receive in life will only speed the procedure up, allowing you to enjoy the benefits of having your wishes realized. Listening to your own voice repeating those desires is quite soothing and also enables you to believe in them completely.

Having said all that, and right before moving on to the powerful manifestations that will speed up the entire process of attracting what you want in life, take a moment to contemplate the following verse: *"As you set out for Ithaca, hope the voyage is a long one, full of adventure and full of discovery"*, as the great Greek poet Constantine P. Cavafy has said (Marlene, 2018). Sometimes, the journey is more important than the destination itself.

MANIFESTING WITH THE MOON PHASES

A spectacular way for you to fulfill your desires in a small time period is to manifest with the moon phases. As you may know, the moon has the ability to control water. We mainly consist of water, which is why we feel so strongly connected to the moon itself. Many people report that they feel influenced by the full moon, and their behavior changes dramatically. It is true that the moon's energy is at its highest peak during the full moon, which is why it takes its toll on everyone on Earth. Besides, a new moon represents a new beginning. A whole new journey starts all over again. This is a clean slate, without blockages in your energy.

In order for you to manifest using the moon phases, you need to write down your wish as it has already happened. As you are well aware of, this is called "living in the present." Unlike projecting a wish to the future, you should make it clear that your wish has been fulfilled. After completing the letter, you should write down the date. This will allow you to be conscious of your desire. You are not vague in wishing for something to happen. Apart from setting a time frame, you also need to be detailed as to how it made you feel. Be very particular, and describe everything. As a consequence, you will enjoy the benefits of exactly what it is that you have wanted to attract in your life.

Visualization is the key to success in manifesting. So, as soon as you have finished writing the letter, you are encouraged to follow a ritual. Bury this piece of paper into the ground. You can choose to bury it in your garden or perhaps in your balcony. Although it might seem strange, placing the paper in the soil will help you stimulate the visualization. It will complete the whole picture, and you will be envisioning that this piece of paper is a seed. This is what connects you to your desire. Let that seed grow and turn into the satisfaction of your desire.

In two weeks, the full moon will take place. Some people will see their wish come true during the full moon. These are the lucky ones! If you are not one of them, do not worry: you just need to write down another letter. This letter will be all about yourself. You will concentrate on your virtues, and write down all the amazing affirmations that describe who you really are. Include things like *"I am loveable," "I am amazing," "My heart is pure gold," "I deserve to be loved," "I deserve to be cherished and respected."* Then, use the very same ritual: bury this piece of paper. Alternatively, you can throw it in the garbage or even flush it down the toilet. But, let us face it, burying it is the best stimulation for your representation of a growing seed.

Waning gibbous is when the moon starts fading away, after the full moon. This is the time for a third letter. In this letter, you will get rid of all the negative emotions you might be experiencing. This time, you will use affirmations, such as *"I release anxiety,"* and *"I release worry,"* so all these self limiting beliefs are gone. Self-limiting affirmations serve a great purpose. They help you change your negative thoughts and prevent any blockage. Unlike the two previous papers, you should burn this one. In this way, you visualize the release of this negative energy. Get rid of it symbolically.

As the moon takes its different shapes, and a full cycle is complete, your desire will soon come true. You can use the energies of the universe in your favor. Achieve the absolute balance with your divine feminine energy, and benefit from this powerful gift you have been given in life. Let nothing hold you back, and make no excuses. You deserve to reach your goals without wasting any more time.

How to Manifest With Water

Have you ever heard of Dr. Masaru Emoto? He was a scientist and became worldwide famous for his water experiments. What he did was place water of the very same source into different jars and then write down different words on these jars. Some words had a positive meaning, such as love or affection. Others were negative emotions, just like hate or disappointment. Afterwards, Dr. Emoto froze the water and observed the jars. What he saw was amazing. The jars containing water and "positive words" had created crystals of immense beauty and symmetry. On the other hand, jars with "negative words" had abnormal-shaped crystals, without any beauty or balance (Pitkanen, 2018). Water holds the vibration of words or anything attached to it.

As mentioned a little earlier in the manifestation using the moon phases, people are mostly made of water. This means that our body gets affected by the moon, as the moon controls water. At the same time, Emoto's experiment has proven that our body is also affected by the vibration of words. Can you fully grasp how huge this realization is? If you are determined to manifest your desire into a month or less, then water manifestation is a great way to do that. You will only need a tall, glass bottle with a cap, a piece of paper, and something to write on it.

On a new moon, it is the best time for you to start this powerful manifestation. However, you can do that whenever you want. Just keep in mind that the new moon reflects new beginnings. You first need to take the paper, and write positive affirmations about your desire. For instance, do you want to get a promotion? Then, start writing about how you feel about having already got that promotion. Remember that you must always write "in the present" and not project your future desires.

What you should be careful of is the particular choice of words you use while journaling. I know that this is oddly specific, but you need to pay attention to the slightest things if you want to be successful in your manifestation. Do not use any word that has been charged with a negative vibe. Rather than saying *"I am not a failure,"* you can try saying *"I am successful, I thrive in what I do."* Even though both sentences have pretty much the same meaning, the first sentence is negatively charged.

Write down your feelings in detail, and be very specific. Take the time to think of all the aspects that are relevant to this promotion. How much money are you going to get? What opportunities will come up eventually? What special perks does this promotion have for you? Before wrapping up the scripting process, be thankful for this desire that you have achieved. Then, get that bottle. Fill it with water, and hold it with both your hands. Have that letter by your side, and start reading each sentence out loud.

As soon as you finish reading each sentence, close your eyes. Repeat the same affirmation over and over again. Do that until you believe that the specific affirmation is true. In this way, you will be transferring your positive vibration to the water bottle. When you are done with one sentence, move on to the next. Once you have finished with the letter, take a sip of the water. As you might have guessed, this water will be charged with the positive vibrations of your entire letter. What a healing potion this is, right?

This sip will remind your body of your desire, and charge it with the positive vibration of your affirmations. Then, place the bottle where it can be charged with the great energy of the new moon. It will absorb this energy, and you can sip on the water for the next month or so. Every time you drink a little water, your body will be energized with this powerful, positive feeling. Do this consistently, and you will fulfill this desire of yours before you know it!

15 DAILY MANIFESTING HABITS TO SHAPE YOUR OUTER REALITY

I t is important to spend your days productively, in a way that enhances your manifesting process. This will allow you to optimize your performance, and attract even more wonderful things into your life. I am sure that you are already on the right track, focusing on how to project into the world all the blessings you want to receive. With the help you get from this book, I am positive that you are going to triumph. However, this does not mean that you should neglect all the other aspects of your life. In fact, there are several habits you can incorporate into your daily routine, in order to lift your spirit and guide you to a new, improved way of living.

Make sure that you commit to this new lifestyle, experimenting with the habits that I have gathered below for you. Even though some of them might appear a little strict, do give them a chance. You will be amazed at the results, since you will shape your outer reality exactly the way you have always hoped for in your dreams. Nothing should hold you back from experiencing the new you: feeling happier, healthier, more accomplished, and wealthier than ever before.

1. Write down notes with your goals, and review them frequently. This is one of the top habits you should

incorporate into your life. Write about everything you want to achieve, and include the date. These can be short-term goals, or life-changing targets. It does not matter if they are important. What matters is that you evaluate your journey, trying to figure out how to make things better for you in the long run. You can use an app in order to keep track more conveniently.

2. Memorize those goals. Of course, I am not saying that you should memorize the entire journal you keep, although that would be impressive! However, you need to repeat the most important goals of yours until you learn them by heart. Then, you will have the opportunity to repeat the goals in your mind again and again. Especially before sleep, it is a great habit to tell yourself all those affirmations that you would like to manifest into your life.

3. Break down the goals you have, and celebrate milestones. It is only fair to break down your goals into smaller ones. For instance, if you want to lose 50 pounds, you cannot have just one goal. Instead, focus on the first milestone of losing 5% of your initial weight. When you do, celebrate it! Reward yourself for your dedication. This will only strengthen your motivation and allow you to continue.

4. Scripting. I have already referred to the power of scripting, or keeping a journal, but I cannot stress that enough. Make it a habit to write down on a daily basis, because it definitely helps you channel your energy. It also allows you to stick to your goals, as it helps you to steer clear of all the temptations to stall. You do not need any delays, do you?

5. Use a vision board. Even if you do not like this in the first place, I assure you that you will be hooked. You know how important visualization can be for manifesting your desires. Use images on a board, where you interpret these desires and shape them into reality. The board can either be of physical form, or digital. Rather than closing your eyes and envisioning those things, open them and enjoy!

6. Listen to meditations or audiobooks, before going to sleep.

There are so many amazing audiobooks out there. Yet, most people are drowned in a hectic lifestyle, with literally no time to dedicate to themselves. Enjoy the productivity, and just relax right before bedtime. All this knowledge will be infused in your mind without you even realizing it.

7. Cultivate a feeling of abundance and practice gratitude. When you feel abundant, you project it to the world, and it comes back to you. This is the concept you want to adhere to when cultivating that feeling of abundance. At the same time, it is equally crucial to practice gratitude. Be thankful for all your blessings, and let the universe know.

8. Smile. As simple as that!

9. Be kind to yourself. Why would you ever want to beat yourself up for something you did? You should cherish who you are, and love yourself beyond limitations.

10. Practice diaphragmatic breathing. Try breathing deeply from your belly. This enables you to use your parasympathetic nervous system, which helps digestion and promotes relaxation.

11. Quit watching TV or at least keep it to a minimum. The time you spend in front of the TV goes to waste. You avoid thinking, and your brain gets overwhelmed by easily digested information and content of no meaning whatsoever. In addition, TV prevents you from indulging in much more beneficial activities; as you know, time is money.

12. Work out regularly. When you work out, you immediately elevate your body's vibration frequency. This alone should motivate you to incorporate a workout routine into your lifestyle. Plus, when you exercise, you release endorphins and feel happy. Your health will be grateful, too!

13. Eat healthy. Your body is a vessel, and you need to treat it with respect. Sometimes we neglect its value, only focusing on our mental clarity and spiritual presence. Choose a viable diet, which not only nourishes your body but also helps it heal. Vegetarianism in all its versions, veganism, paleo diet, or the Mediterranean diet: these are all great options for

you to experiment with, always with respect to seasonality and local produce.

14. Connect with nature. It is a magnificent privilege to go out in nature and truly align with its grandeur. Go out for a walk, taking in the fresh air while listening to the birds chirping. Smell the aromas of the blossomed flowers, look at the chromatic combinations in the fields, or up in the sky. Enjoy a lovely sunrise or a captivating sunset. There are so many things that will bring balance between you, and your surroundings.

15. Wake up early in the morning. Last but not least, you should at least try to be an early bird. When you wake up early, you have more time to devote to things that will improve your quality of life. Have a long shower, meditate, or prepare a healthy breakfast. Give yourself the time you need to wake up smoothly, awaken your senses with a sip of your favorite beverage, and prepare your mind and body for a day filled with energy.

That is it! Of course, you are most welcome to add more positive habits that contribute to the advancement of your manifestation experience. Focus on what makes you feel good deep inside, since this is what you are going to emit. In return, happiness attracts happiness. Joy sparks joy and returns in multitude. Love, affection, affluence, success, or growth: you name it!

RELEASE RESISTANCE WHEN EXPECTING MANIFESTATIONS

You have started this wonderful journey towards reaching your higher self and manifesting your desires into the world. During this journey, you have been through some truly groundbreaking changes in your life. You have learned how to relax and avoid negative thoughts. In addition, you have mastered the art of manifesting a specific emotion or a particular person. You have been through the ups and downs of this amazing experience, and now you are ready to enjoy the benefits of manifestation in all its glory.

However, there is a fear growing deep inside you. Although it has begun as a tiny sliver of doubt, it has now gone out of proportion. All these expectations that you have when it comes to manifesting might sound natural to you. Nonetheless, they can transform from motivational patterns into the cause of your frustration. Does that seem contradictory? Well, there is a fine line here and this is what I want to discuss. Expectations are typically strong beliefs that you have about something, which you are certain is going to happen. For example, one of your expectations can be to become abundant in life. You are sure it is on its way, and this makes you feel awesome.

A specific time passes by, and you have not reached the point where you feel abundance flowing into your life. Even though the expectations of wealth gave you joy in the past, it is now starting to threaten you. More than that, you are beginning to question the effectiveness of your behavior. *"Am I doing this the right way?"*, *"Why is manifesting not working for me?"*, *"What is wrong with me?"*, and *"How long do I still have to wait until I get what I deserve in life?"* These are just a few of the questions that might be crawling into your mind, causing you extreme discomfort.

If your expectations are causing you frustration, then they build up resistance. Therefore, you need to release that. It is hurting you, while at the same time blocking your progress towards fulfilling your goals. I know that I may have touched a chord with this description, but it is best to deal with it as soon as it occurs. Rather than settling for a constant feeling of stress, you need to relax. You need to release the tension, which is caused by resistance. What you ought to do is switch your mindset to hope. Do not worry about how you can achieve that. It is quite simple, yet truly effective as a strategy.

Expecting something to happen means that you are counting backwards until it does happen. This might trigger anticipation beyond the point you can handle. As a result, it brings you anxiety and eventually leads to disappointment. You cannot spend your days concerned as to why your desire has not manifested yet. This is counterproductive, and offers no real benefit to you. On the other hand, you can reverse the situation pretty easily. What you do is concentrate on the feeling of expectation, hoping for your desire to manifest promptly. Does that sound hard?

This shift in your mindset will reflect on your daily affirmations, too. You will no longer think of the following: *"I expect my desire to manifest. Why hasn't it already manifested? I must be doing something wrong."* Instead, you will have more positive thoughts: *"I hope that my desire manifests. I hope that I am doing everything right, and my desire manifests soon."* Although these two attitudes bear some resemblance, the truth is that they are very different. The first one adds stress in the mix, whereas the second soothes your soul, filling you with a positive vibe.

Practice Makes Perfect

It would be spectacular to change your life from one moment to the next. Unfortunately, this is not how life works. Where would the fun be in that? If you were able to transform your life so easily, it would not feel that great to accomplish one of your goals. It would be just a mere part of reality, something that would happen either way. *"No pain, no gain"* as I am sure you have heard numerous times before. Nevertheless, this does not mean that you should not try to improve your existence and attract everything you want to receive.

This is what the Law of Attraction does, giving you a helping hand to reach the goals that you have set for yourself. It goes without even saying that you cannot expect to fulfill these goals overnight. Take for instance the list I have shared with you containing 15 daily manifestation habits that will work wonders for you. This is great, and you should definitely start ticking those habits. Yet, can you do all of these things? Are you sure? Even if you can, how long do you think it will take you?

Start slow, and work yourself up the ladder, adding more into the mix when you feel more comfortable. In this case, you can start by smiling more every day and following a healthy diet. You can also engage in physical activity by walking to and from the office. Buy a journal, and start documenting your days. Figure out the positive affirmations that work for you, so as to memorize and repeat on a daily basis. Cut down on the time you spend in front of the TV, and instead go out and admire nature.

Gradually build your life in the way that makes you happier and more satisfied. Take comfort as you realize how much you have grown, realizing exactly what matters in life, and putting all the toxic thoughts aside. Even if you fall off the wagon, never beat yourself up over this. Regard it as a small obstacle, which will only make you stronger. Do not consider it the tip of the iceberg, since this will bring you a great deal of stress for the future.

Consistency is vital in this endeavor. You will need to commit to your efforts, and follow your habits for the long run. Otherwise, all your hard labor will go to waste. By being consistent, you increase your chances of success. Remember that you want to change the vibration frequency of your body. The best way to do so is by emitting positive energy from within, and you can only succeed in that through long-term changes in the way you feel. Stick to this regime, and watch the benefits as they present themselves to you.

☙ 10 ❧

MANIFESTATION
SKYROCKETING
MEDITATIONS

Are you ready for some powerful, calming, and upbeat guided manifesting for women meditations? In this section of the book, I am going to show you exactly how you can meditate, in order to attract the specific things you want in your life. These meditations will show you how to focus on what is most important to you. They are outlined in detail for your optimal convenience. I have made sure to include step-by-step meditations that cover everything you need so that you can record the text from the book and listen back to it as a guided meditation if you want. How about it?

Remember that you need to focus on a single goal every time you manifest. If you get super excited—and include multiple wishes in your manifestation—then you are about to experience some serious disappointment. The truth is that the manifestation gets split many ways if you have more than one desire added in the mix. As a result, the energy you emit will not draw the results that you are anticipating. To avoid all that discomfort, it is best to concentrate on a single goal. In this way, you will be able to achieve that faster, and far more efficiently.

MEDITATION TO MANIFEST ANYTHING

As the title suggests, this is a flexible meditation that can be used pretty much for anything you wish to attract.

Take a deep breath. This is the time to clear your mind of every other thought. Let go of the physical world. Just focus on the thing you want to attract in your life. Manifesting can be relevant to anything in life. However, you need to be extra specific.

Do not be afraid of specifying exactly what it is that you want to manifest. Is it to earn $20,000 by the end of the month? Or is it to get your ex back within the next 10 days? Maybe your wish is to get healthier and lower your cholesterol levels as soon as possible. Do you want to attract a successful associate to join your business by the end of this term? Think of every single detail, and avoid being vague.

Breathe deeply again, feeling absolutely relaxed. As you are relaxing, you can access your deeper spirit more easily. You open up, and believe in this meditation. Remember that you are already experiencing what you want to manifest. Believe in that, as you are taking another deep breath.

You are now feeling your body letting go of every single muscle. Your muscles become loose and they are falling down beneath you, starting from your legs. Your belly is relaxed, and the tension on your neck escapes you. You relax your jaw and these muscles around your eyes. Your whole body experiences that calmness and lightness in your life.

Take another deep breath, and try to notice any negative feeling. I am sure that there are still persistent emotions that prevent you from reaching out to your divine feminine energy. Let go of every negative feeling, like fear, doubt, or depression. Replace these feelings with positive energy flowing through your entire body.

Now, concentrate on what you want to manifest. How would you feel if you already had that in your life? How would this affect your life? Would it also change the lives of those around you? Imagine all the consequences of this manifestation.

Take a moment to visualize how you introduce that to those within your circle of family and friends. Imagine their reactions, and visualize your discussions with them. You are already seeing it unfold before your eyes.

Envision your life as you are enjoying this manifestation in your life. Sense it: feel it in your core. See your life now after having attracted this desire in your life, and focus on the feelings you experience. Are you happy? Does this make you feel more motivated? This is already happening in the present—there is no doubt about it.

You have no restrictions, so it does not make any difference how this manifestation came to be. It is thanks to your limitless possibilities that you have attracted it into your life, and now you are enjoying all the benefits surrounding it. You have what you want right now, and this is all that matters. This is your reality; this is your moment to shine.

Continue with your visualization. You can see it right before your eyes, so you know it is there. If it is not physical, you are seeing the reactions of that desire manifested in your life, so there is no doubt for you that it has happened.

Now let it go: let all these positive feelings and visualizations go. Do not worry: you are not going to lose your manifestation. This will allow you to take action and manifest this desire in your life for good. Every decision you make will bring you closer to your goal.

Take a deep breath and relax. You know that your subconscious will guide you, so that you effortlessly receive what you want. This is your belief—no one can take it away from you. Breathe deeply and return back to reality, knowing that your manifestation is on its way.

Shifting Your Reality

If you want to attract great things in life, you need to change your frequency. This is a wonderful meditation which will help you shift your vibration, and in turn allow you to manifest everything in your life.

This is a powerful meditation that will transform your life and your entire physical presence. Get comfortable: laying down somewhere cozy.

Take three deep breaths, inhaling through the nose and exhaling through mouth. This will help you relax, soothe your senses completely, and prepare to shift your frequencies.

Imagine your thoughts and the tension of your day slowly fading away, so that you are light and calm. Then, visualize an abundant light. Start relaxing your feet and your ankles, going up to your thighs and your belly.

Move upwards, allowing every cell in your body to absorb the wonderful light that you are visualizing. Continue all the way up to your chest, your neck, and now your face. The light is shining on your beautiful face and now above your head.

Now, visualize two pairs of shoes. The ones on the left reflect your old self. They are worn out, and they look unappealing. The shoes on the right represent your new self, so you want to walk on these new shoes.

Imagine that you are walking towards your manifestation. Your desire has already come true, so you are enjoying this walk on your new shoes, feeling wonderful. How does this make you feel? Experience this entire process in detail.

What does this manifestation feel like? What changes have taken place? See them vividly. Expand on this feeling even more. Allow this warm feeling envelope itself through your body. How do you feel?

You have already received your manifestation. Observe the reactions of those around you, and interpret your own behavior. Allow yourself to soak in this experience, as you are enjoying every single aspect of this manifestation in your life. What other opportunities does this bring?

See the changes on the new you, as you are growing more mature, more intelligent, and more accomplished. You are living your dream. You are the best version of yourself. All your desires are taking place before your eyes, and you are feeling great. You are feeling complete.

Take a last deep breath, and remember your new you. Get used to this feeling, as this is going to attract everything you want in your life. Repeat the same meditation as often as you like, at least daily for a whole month. Open your eyes, stretch a little, and smile.

MEDITATION TO MANIFEST A LOVING RELATIONSHIP

If you want to attract love into your life, then you should follow this powerful meditation. It will help you open up and get ready to connect to the world.

Take a deep breath, and make sure that you are in the moment. Lift your chest so that your lungs expand. Fill your lungs with fresh air as much as you can. Hold that air for a little while, and breathe out gently. Repeat the same thing twice.

Surrender your body weight to the surface underneath you, and feel yourself becoming lighter. Feel your energy flow gently. Breath effortlessly, and visualize two roses side-by-side. Notice the colors of these roses and the texture of their petals.

See these roses clearly, keeping your eyes closed. Take one of these two roses, and keep it in the palm of your hand. Offer it as a gift to your heart. Be kind and gentle. Watch it fill the space within your heart. It has blossomed, opening up to your chest.

This is a reminder of the fact you need to love yourself. Admire this rose of deep love. It represents who you are, along with your tenderness, your honesty, and your ability to connect deeply with those around you. It shows that you can connect even with those who you have not met yet.

Think of the warmth of your smile and the softness of your touch. You are unique, with innate goodness showering those around you. Remind yourself, if you do not already know, that you are a true blessing to this world.

Now go ahead,m and visualize the second rose. Observe it carefully, looking at each little detail. It is delicate and fresh. If you look closer, you will realize the second rose is unique, too. This will bring a loving, caring partner in your life.

Feel your desire to love and be loved: you are worthy of experiencing this feeling. Congratulate yourself on your courage for loving and supporting yourself. You should be happy, because you want to show affection to another person.

You are enjoying a unique bond with your partner, and this is your honest intention. See the two roses merging at the center of your heart. This connection has been accomplished. The two flowers commit to loving yourself fully, while also welcoming the love of your partner. It is a wonderful feeling deriving from your pure intention.

The universe is guiding you always, leading you towards a person who nurtures you, loves you, respects you, and accepts who you really are. A person who cherishes every moment they spend with you, and loves you unconditionally.

Visualize the two roses again: repeat the same meditation every time you wish to attract love into your life. Breathe deeply again, and concentrate on your body. Feel your body becoming grounded again, and softly open your eyes.

Meditation to Attract Success in Life

This is a great meditation which will welcome success into your life. It is mainly used to attract wealth and business accomplishments.

You must keep your body grounded, so you need to find a position where you sit comfortably. Your feet are on the ground, and your shoulders are relaxed, looking down. Breathe deeply and slowly.

Take a moment and bring thoughts of success to mind. Visualize that, indulging in the greatest expressions of success. Your mind can dive right in the most glorious moments of success, and bring them before your eyes.

You should be proud of what you have accomplished so far, given these moments of success that come to mind. Now is the time for you to take full control of your life, enhancing success.

This is the time to start doing all the things that you have been postponing. No more struggles, no more anxiety, and no more stress as you are letting go of your past habits and incorporating new ones into your life. You are ready to take the next step toward success. You are ready for positive habits, such as getting more organized.

In the past, you have procrastinated. Putting off projects, avoiding work, and making bad choices is no longer an option. Now, you are ready to create the foundation for a positive life.

Take a deep breath, and expand your chest. Breathe deeply and slowly again. You have realized that you must take care of some unpleasant things and tackle them with mastery. This is the only way for you to succeed in your adult life. Do not avoid the tasks that you did not favor in the past.

Do not let your ego take control, as you are ready to get into the path of success. Get rid of all the negative thoughts and projections. This will allow the positive energy to flow through your body and into your daily life.

What are the habits that you want to incorporate into your life? Visualize them in detail, so as to experience them and make a difference in your success journey. Do you want to commit to waking up early or tackling the accounting of your business? Turn these thoughts into habits.

You are ready to experience a sense of freedom as you grow stronger emotionally, and mentally. This is the path towards success for you. Everyday the work becomes easier to accomplish, and you thrive pursuing new positive habits.

Make a pledge that you will adhere to your new commitments, no matter how difficult they might be. This is the way to reach greatness, so you are determined to succeed. Your success will come naturally, freely, and effortlessly.

Breathe deeply again, and slowly regain consciousness of your body. You have remained grounded, so open your eyes, and welcome your new reality. Welcome to the path of success.

11

MANIFESTING ROAD BLOCKS AND HOW TO CRUSH THEM

"*Why is the Law of Attraction not working for me?*"—This is probably the most frequently asked question and paints a picture I feel the need to explain further. It is true that not all people who practice the Law of Attraction see results. Or to be more precise, they do not see them unless they realize what they have been doing wrong. If you want to be successful in this path to attracting all the things you want in your life, you need to study. It is essential that you fully comprehend the science behind the Law of Attraction.

I have explained the basic principles of the Law of Attraction earlier in my book. Basically, you need to understand that vibration attracts vibration, and every person has their own resonant frequency. When you reach that resonant frequency, you can literally succeed in anything. What you ought to do is to change your vibrational frequency and your thought patterns so that you align yourself to what you want. Universe works with time and space. Therefore, you need to constantly align to that vibrational frequency. Otherwise, you will not be able to attract it into your life.

That being said, we are only human. This means that we are bound to make mistakes. A negative thought, a period of feeling under the weather, or a panic attack: these can cause blockages and hinder your progress while trying to manifest your wishes. It is only fair that you realize what these obstacles really are in order to deal with them efficiently. How do you know what your blockages are; how can you get rid of these blockages in your way to manifest your desires into the world?

You attract more of what you feel, rather than what you think of at a time. The universe will pick up on why you want something in your life. If you are manifesting something because of a certain lack, the universe will disprove you, and you will end up without getting what you want. This is why it is crucial that you feel abundance, so as to attract affluence right back at you. Try to feel the fulfillment. Your emotions and your thoughts are the ones that are shaping your reality: it is not the other way around.

Trying to make something happen is very masculine, and this is great on several occasions. However, this does not work well in your love life—think of it that way. When you are trying to visualize your dream partner, you should focus on allowing them to come into your life. This is where you would like to shift to your feminine energy. Otherwise, you would be starting from a position of lack. You want to manifest your dream partner, because you do not have them. This is going to be catastrophic for you. When it comes to matters of the heart, you ought to bring out your feminine energy. This will help you set the tone for welcoming what you already visualize into your life.

Another blockage that you may not even think of is the impact of your manifestations to others. Although you would think they do not really affect your manifestation, they actually do. Imagine that you want to travel the world and discover different cultures. This is a marvelous opportunity for you, filling you with excitement and joy. How about your overprotective parents, though, or your loving partner? Do they share your enthusiasm, or is this manifestation going to bring out negative emotions?

What you need to do in this case is to reinterpret the negative consequences of your manifested desire into empowering beliefs. You should make sure that your manifestation sparks joy on everyone else, which is how the universe will grant you your wish. For example, you can visualize that you communicate with your parents frequently, and that they are proud of you for pursuing your goals. Maybe you struggle with that reinterpretation at first. This will only get better over time, since your brain will gradually be rewired into thinking positively. Not only that, but your subconscious brain will follow the same path.

Changing your mind too often will prevent you from manifesting what you want. This happens because you want so many different things, and you do not allow yourself enough time to process and align to that particular vibrational frequency to attract it. Do not just move on, but instead find what you actually want. Stick to that goal, and do not let go until it has indeed manifested. Then you can of course pursue something different. However, do not confuse the universe like that, and do not lose focus.

Before completing this reference of road blocks that you might encounter during manifesting, you should clarify the difference between meditation and focused visualization. Unless you realize how to use either of these techniques, you may block your progress when manifesting. So, through meditation, you use mindfulness to gain awareness. You basically shift your mindset, trying to reach mental clarity and a calm state of mind. On the other hand, focused visualization allows you to focus on what you want to attract. It is more straightforward and can be done anytime. You simply get rid of distractions, and concentrate on the one thing you want to achieve.

DOES YOUR PERSONAL INTEGRITY GET IN THE WAY?

In or out of integrity? You cannot fake the Law of Attraction.

Integrity is your set of principles: your moral code that drives you to behave in a specific way. Every single time you do something that is not in alignment with your core values, you feel negative vibrations. This in turn leads to obstacles in your path towards manifesting your desires into reality. Does that sound like something you want in your life? This is a rhetorical question, since I know how devoted you are towards manifesting and reaching your higher self.

There is an antidote, which can be used to counteract this particular poison. Be honest, pay your debts, and avoid borrowing things from others. Be kind to people around you, and never gossip about them. Never make a promise that you do not intend to keep. Be punctual and fair in your decisions. Everything you say and do should be guided by these values. Do not fall into the vortex of telling lies, even if you consider them "white lies" or innocent. Even these lies will keep you from achieving your goals. The pure positive energy that you want into your life will be hindered.

It is important that you are true to yourself. Otherwise, you will be facing a moral dilemma. Even if you try to rationalize, you can never justify your actions by bending the truth. Just visualize that you are in the other person's shoes, the person you have been affecting with your behavior. How would you feel if something similar happened to you? If there was a person who behaved in a similar manner to you, would you be content? Or would you feel frustrated and out of place?

We all make mistakes, and this is pretty understandable. You cannot always be in control of your every thought, and you can expect to be tempted once every now and then. The world is a challenging place, after all. Every day, you interact with people. You make decisions about everything, from the smallest thing to the most important milestone. Remember that you are not in a contest: this is your life you are trying to optimize. After having slipped through a slippery slope of lies and dishonesty, you are going to make your life a lot more difficult.

What you need to commit to is personal accountability. When you always make up excuses about behaving badly, you do that to feel better with your particular choices. Yet, this does not work well in the long run. After a while, you will notice the change in your frequency vibration. Your entire balance will be crushed, leaving you hanging.

Even if you are doing everything else right, you will not get to see the results that you have anticipated through your manifesting journey.

Redeem yourself by doing your best to maintain the balance in the world. You cannot change your past—this is non-negotiable. However, through redeeming, you will change your vibration while doing something nice to another person; this will allow your vibration to shift. It is a constant struggle, and you must be aware of the hardships. However, you should never behave in a way that harms others. This is the epitome of dropping your vibration and damaging your psyche. How can you anticipate to manifest after that?

Five Harmful Myths About Manifesting That Might Be Hurting You

It makes sense that you dig deeper into the Law of Attraction and the concept of manifesting your desires into the world. There is a plethora of information out there, so it is very easy for you to reach out and gather a multitude of resources to study. However, you should take everything with a grain of salt. In other words, do not just fall for every single video you watch on YouTube.

Do not believe in everything you hear, especially if that contradicts your existing beliefs or your knowledge on the matter. Believe me, sometimes less is more. Below, I am going to refer to five of the most dangerous myths out there about manifesting. The reason I am doing it is to protect you, and motivate you to cross-check everything you learn about the Law of Attraction.

One of my personal favorites is the myth of "If/then." There are people claiming that you can manifest every single desire and get it with no questions asked. The only requirement is that you put the "If/then" rule into effect. This holds a deeper fear, though: I am talking about the exoneration trap. Life is filled with challenges. In order to achieve something, people need to dedicate time and effort. Dissatisfaction and not having the things we want is a part of our lives. Sometimes, when something you want does not manifest into your life, then this is a lesson from the universe. You should not think of it as a punishment. Being disappointed over having to struggle for something is counterproductive and totally distorts you from appreciating the true meaning of life.

Moving on, there is the misconception that you can manifest things, even when you are not ready to receive them in your life. This could not be further from the truth, though. You need to become the right person, in order to get the right things. Let me give you an example. If someone gets a million dollars, without having worked a single day in their life, then they are clueless as to how to invest that money. They have not gone through the process of earning the money, learning how to form a fruitful business, and so on. As a result, they basically live on borrowed time, and end up being broke. What is the point of receiving a blessing when you are clearly not ready to receive it at the specific time?

Another myth that might get in the way, and potentially harm you in your effort to manifest your desire into your life, is oversharing. I know that you are overly enthusiastic about the Law of Attraction. This is amazing, and I would like nothing more than to see your expectations met and even exceeded along the way. However, there is a thin line you should never cross. When you tell others what you are attempting to do, you are risking the possibility of attracting negative emotions. If they are jealous of your manifested success and happiness, they will project that negative energy to you. Are you sure you want that in your life?

You do not need to become secretive. Just filter the things you share, so as to maintain a balanced social life without any glitches along the way. I am not saying that you should become an introvert, or lie to people. In fact, I have explained how lies can have a negative effect on your manifestations. Nevertheless, there is no reason why others should know the slightest detail about how you have accomplished so much. Obviously, they do not have to know how much money you have in the bank and how the Law of Attraction has helped you in that. This can save you from a lot of pain: trust me.

The fourth myth about the Law of Attraction is definitely the fraction of time it takes in order to achieve your goals. Tell me honestly: how can you expect to bring something so wonderful into your life overnight? The claims are literally preposterous. It is exactly like claiming that a specific diet is going to help you lose 30 pounds in a single week. These claims cannot be validated, of course, and they mess with your determination. Once you see that you do not fulfill these manifestations in a short amount of time, it makes sense to get discouraged. Disbelief creeps in your mind and prevents your growth.

Finally, a myth that is constantly repeating itself about manifesting is the obsession over materialistic possessions. Many people think that getting money or a fancy house, will automatically erase any negative emotions they have. I wish things were that simple! Under no circumstances should you idolize money or possessions. They should not be your objective rather than a means to achieve what you want. The only thing that they can provide is peace of mind as to your financial future. They enable you to do more, but it is up to you how to handle the resources you receive.

As you can see, there are several misconceptions that can actually hinder you from your opportunity to shine and reach your personal goals. Set rational targets, and always evaluate the things that you read about or listen to in a podcast, a video, or a conversation. Have faith in your own power, and do whatever makes you happy without messing with your body's vibrational frequency. Now let us move forward to the final chapter of this book, where I lay out an inspiring daily ritual to help you manifest.

12

THE 30-MINUTE FEMININE
MANIFESTATION DAILY
RITUAL SECRET FORMULA

I t is important that you follow a daily ritual, which will allow you to start your day productively, feeling amazing. This is how to set the tone for your high vibrational frequency in order to attract what it is you want to manifest in your life. Of course, you can add your personal touches and make the perfect morning ritual to adhere to every single day. Wake up early in the morning, as this will allow you to appreciate nature at its finest moment. It is calm outside, as the world has not started its frenzy. You wake up and get ready for a full day of excitement. Making your bed will give you a sense of accomplishment, and this is a wonderful feeling to hold on to throughout the day. Write your own routine and stick it on your wall for inspiration: it works!

As soon as you wake up, you should open your curtains, and let that natural light bathe the room. This is a symbolic way to cleanse and purify the environment you are in, while at the same time lifting your spirit up high. Open the windows, and take in a deep breath of fresh air. That feels rejuvenating, right? Of course, it is all a matter of where you live. If you are in the countryside, or if you have a garden, you will smell the blossomed flowers and even listen to the birds chirping happily. Even if you are not, though, it does not matter. Appreciate where you are, and be in the moment.

Keep your home clean and decluttered. I cannot stress that enough. Your personal space is a reflection of what goes on inside you, which means that a cluttered home means you are a mess. How can you stand this chaotic situation? On the other hand, if you clean up on a regular basis, everything will be neatly stored. This will allow you to feel better, projecting it to the world around you. In a similar pattern, pay attention to your personal hygiene and the way you look. It has nothing to do with vanity. However, you should cherish yourself and treat you like the goddess you really are.

Now is the time to move on to the actual morning ritual, which will offer you the opportunity to expand your manifestation. It will not take more than 30 minutes, which is absolutely great. This is adequate time for you to dedicate to yourself, promoting your self-growth and ensuring that you are on the right track towards happiness, abundance, and love.

1. After waking up, you should take some time to focus on your breathing. This is a great way to calm your mind down and restore that perfect balance in your body. Breathe through the nose, and exhale through the mouth. Instead of the hectic breathing you have been accustomed to, try abdominal breathing. As a result, you will feel your lungs filled with air in their maximum capacity. Release the air back into the atmosphere gently. Now, cover one of your

nostrils and breathe through the other one. Even if you do not know this, we always use a single nostril to breathe in and out. This nostril shifts after a few hours. So controlling your breathing like that enables you to relax even further. You calm the mind, set your intention, trust in the universe, and allow things to flow into our lives

2. Then, it is time to be thankful. Dedicate just five minutes for a gratitude meditation. Keep a gratitude journal, where you express your gratitude for all the blessings that you already have in your life. Use "as/if" sentences, in order to enhance this feeling of self-accomplishment. Close your eyes, and think about all the things you are grateful for in your life. You are healthy, you have a roof over your head, and you are surrounded by loving family and friends. It can be anything, as long as you feel grateful. Along with what you have already accomplished in life, you should also include the things you want to attract. These are things you need to draw closer to you, so make sure that you give thanks about already having them. This will create the perfect frequency, so that you can attract them promptly towards you. Do not forget to smile, as this is basically the manifestation of your happiness.

3. Devote some time to write daily in a journal, practicing your scripting. This is where you need to include your personal affirmations, which will boost your confidence and keep you motivated. Read through the affirmations that you have already written down, and leave the journal somewhere you can access very easily. Take some moments to repeat these affirmations out loud. When you do, you will immediately feel your spirit lift. You want that in your life. Obviously, you can practice scripting throughout the day, or even right before going to sleep. Nevertheless, early in the morning this activity will give you the energy boost you need for the day.

4. After having focused on your mental tasks, it is time to

remove the stagnant energy. You need to get active. I would suggest engaging in a yoga session or pilates; however, it is totally up to you. If you feel like it, you can dance to the beat of your favorite music. Alternatively, you can stretch and do some cardio. Getting on your treadmill is a great way to feel the energy flow through your body while increasing your vibrational frequency. It goes without even saying that activities outdoors are even better. If the weather is fine, go out for a walk or a jog.

5. Next, head to the bathroom. It is your time to relax and wash away all the negative thoughts that have been running through your mind. Take a shower, feeling the healing properties of the water. Enjoy the relaxing atmosphere, as you are soothing your muscles and awakening your senses fully. Then, apply your makeup. Do whatever makes you feel beautiful as you truly are. Be radiant with a glow that starts from within, as you present yourself as your best version. Finally, do not forget to smile! Pick the clothes you are going to wear and get ready.

6. Last but not least, prepare a healthy breakfast. Start your day eating wholesome foods, without any process. You can have a smoothie, or a fruit salad. Be sure to include superfoods, which allow you to get your omega-3s, antioxidants, and vitamins for the day. Chia seeds, flaxseed, avocado, or berries: these are all excellent foods to start your day with, along with some herbal tea or coffee. This is where you can relax and maybe go through your emails, or scroll through your social media accounts. Listen to some music, and make plans for the rest of your day.

Now you are perfectly aligned to the energy of the universe, looking forward to attracting all the things you want to receive in your life. Good morning, sunshine!

SAVE TIME BY MAKING ONE SMALL CHANGE IN YOUR MANIFESTING ROUTINE

What you want is to amplify your positive energy and empower your manifestation. rather than spending endless hours trying to make things work, you need to focus on what enhances your efforts. There are several things that you can do so as to minimize the time it takes for your manifesting routine to get into motion. You can use scented candles when meditating, or you may indulge in the power of herbs. However, if I had to pick just one thing to optimize your manifesting routine, that would be the use of crystals.

When crystals are used in your manifestation, they will boost your energy beyond compare. Although everything in the universe has its own vibration, there are items such as crystals that hold a much more powerful vibration. Therefore, they have the potential to amplify your intentions and project them to the world. This is what you want to achieve. Get the best results, dedicating the least time possible to receive them. Below, I have handpicked three crystals that are my favorite. All of them are perfect to use in your manifestations, as long as you respect their special characteristics.

Amethyst is an extraordinary crystal, which allows you to connect deeply to the source energy. You want that when you are trying to manifest your desires. Amethyst is a wonderful option, because it boosts your inner confidence and also soothes your senses. Amethyst is responsible for promoting your spiritual enlightenment, as it is aligned with the third eye chakra. By using amethyst in your manifestations, you purify the negativism around you, and you protect your energy preservation.

Rose quartz is another crystal that will help you when manifesting love, as it is called "the love stone" for a reason. This crystal is aligned with your heart chakra. If you have gone through a traumatic experience, rose quartz will empower your healing. When you are in a relationship, it makes sense that you use the rose quartz. This special crystal will enable you to attract compassion, love, and affection, bringing down the walls some people build in their heart. These are the attributes of a perfect relationship, right? If you do not have a relationship just yet, try placing the rose quartz underneath your bed and see what happens.

Finally, perhaps the best crystal to use to optimize your manifesting journey is citrine. Not only does it increase optimism, but it is also great for mental clarity and abundance. You would want a crystal that removes toxins: in a world where we are surrounded by toxic thoughts and people, this is of paramount importance. Remove all this negativism, and set your mind out for success. Now, in order for you to step into your personal power and build your confidence even more, you should use citrine. This crystal is connected to your solar plexus, which strengthens your intuition.

Obviously, you can experiment with many different crystals. There are wonderful precious items out there, including black obsidian, pyrite, green aventurine, and green jade. Moreover, you can go for the yellow sapphire, topaz, zircon, ruby, and hematite, just to name a few. As long as you read through the crystal's properties, you will be able to use them to your advantage. If you cannot decide, then you can mix them up together. In fact, some crystals work extremely well in combination.

Apart from buying these crystals, you need to know how to use them. First and foremost, you should cleanse the crystal thoroughly. You do not know where the crystal has been and who it has been used by. You should cleanse it out of any negative, stagnant energy. You can do that by taking it out in nature, possibly washing it in the crystalline waters of a small stream. This will also absorb the energy and life of nature. Of course, you can also clean it using running water at home. In addition, you can use Himalayan salt.

Next step is for you to charge the crystal you have just bought. Place it out under the moonlight, ideally during full moon. Be careful not to leave the crystal out in the sun, as its color will fade away. This applies to all crystals, not only citrine. Last, you need to consecrate on the crystal; in other words, you need to set your intentions. To do that properly, you must be well aware of the crystal's properties. Now you are ready to connect with the crystal on a deeper level. Hold it in your hands and bring it closer to your solar plexus. Close your eyes, maintaining high vibrations and a clear, pure mind. This is when you are expected to focus on what you want to manifest. Let your crystal know about it.

Nighttime Ritual

Have you ever considered sleep as a super long meditation session? Sleep enables your body to reset and get ready for another day filled with possibilities. Sometimes, people are so exhausted that they get in bed and fall asleep instantly. A minute has passed, maybe even less, and they are out—sleeping like babies. However, others experience trouble sleeping due to stress and too many thoughts flooding their brain. We need to face it: sleep is too long to endure negative energy.

This is why you need to take some time and engage in a simple, yet soothing nighttime ritual. You will feel lighter, and you will focus on what actually matters. There is no point in losing sleep, worrying about things that you cannot control. On the contrary, you can use sleep as a means to manifest. How about it? When sleeping, you get in direct contact with your subconscious brain. So, if you can channel your desires in a way that allows them to reach your subconscious, then you will be successful in your manifestation. It is definitely worth giving this a try. I promise you, it will change the way you feel and manifest!

First of all, prepare a soothing hot beverage. A cup of tea, like chamomile, will allow you to calm down. If you want, you can warm some milk. Do some stretching, and relax your muscles. Your body needs to feel free and light. By stretching, you release any tension from the body. This will prevent cramps or any other discomforting feelings that may disturb your sleep. Then, listen to a motivational podcast or a video filled with positive stuff that you can use as a source of inspiration. A guided meditation will get you primed and relax you deeply.

Clear out all the thoughts you have and all the stumbles that you may have encountered through the day. I am sure you have a lot on your plate but try to compartmentalize. Right before bedtime, you do not need to worry over things that you have no control over: this does not get you anywhere. It will only mess with your tranquility and most likely lead to a sleepless night. What you ought to do is amplify positive emotions, so as to shower yourself with them. They will guide you towards scripting. Talk yourself off the emotional ledge you have found yourself on, to help you find relief. Practice gratitude, as it naturally shifts us into a positive vibrational frequency. All that creates a positive wave of momentum in your life.

Of course, you should steer clear of technology before bed. Although swiping on your mobile phone might seem tempting, this will fill your mind with information to manifest. At least one hour before sleeping, lock these devices away and out of your reach. If you need extra motivation to do that, think of how the blue light emitted from these devices takes its toll on your body. It decreases the rate of producing melatonin, which is responsible for regulating sleep through controlling your circadian rhythm. Why would you deliberately mess with that?

Another thing you need to consider before sleeping is to meditate. It does not have to be sophisticated, or take up a lot of your precious time. You purely practice your breathing, so as to relax and eventually reach nothingness. Witness your senses, without any dialogue. Feel the breath, take in the smell, and listen to the sound of silence. This is the secret that will allow you to meditate properly. After having completed your meditation, you can now move forward with your focused visualization. As I mentioned earlier in the book, meditation enables you to maintain your calmness. Visualization, on the other hand, helps you focus on the one desire you want to manifest.

Finally, let go. Stop thinking. As you already know, the Law of Attraction does not work with expectations. Instead of attaching your self to something, you need to detach. So, after having set your phones aside, after having listened to an inspirational video while sipping on jasmine tea or after having meditated and visualized your desires, now it is time to let go. Repeat the following lines, and stop thinking about anything: *"Universe, I am grateful for everything in my life. What will be, will be."*

AFTERWORD

I am so happy to see that you have completed reading my book on manifesting for women. I am so proud of you for reaching into your spiritual self and doing your best to improve your life on so many different levels. You deserve to be happy; therefore, you need to put theory into practice, and set out on this wonderful journey of the senses. Hopefully, this has been an eye-opening experience for you, clarifying all the things that you may not have truly comprehended up until this moment.

The Law of Attraction is a precious gift handed over to you generously so as to change your life. You need to stay focused, and study all the aspects of how to make it work for you based on your own specialized requirements. Now that you have covered the principles of how manifesting works through reading my book, you are ready to transform your existence, and enjoy all the blessings that you have been desiring to receive. This is a spectacular opportunity for you, and you need to dive right in to relish all those glorious benefits ahead.

You have already taken the first step. Congratulations are in order for taking initiative and getting all the way through this book! This was a fantastic idea, and you have so many wonderful things to look forward to now that you have read through these pages. I will be right there by your side throughout your endeavors: offering my advice to you and supporting your ventures 100%. It is an exciting time that unveils before you, and I am sure that you already have a huge smile on your face.

Remember to love yourself, and believe that you can accomplish everything you set your mind on as long as you align to the energy of the universe. Tune in the frequency you emit so that you attract the exact same things that you want, leaving all those toxic thoughts and people out of reach. They do not belong in your reality—what they do is bring you down and distract you from your path. You do not want that: you do not have the time to withhold your manifestations.

Moving forward, I would suggest that you take some time to let all this information sink in. After that, lay out your strategy. Plan your next steps, in order for you to remain organized in your manifesting routine. Make use of the meditations that I have shared with you, and experiment with different techniques. This is the best way to see what appeals to you the most. Whatever you do, always keep in mind that the sky's the limit. The universe is always listening: thus, you should connect with the world, and let abundance overflow your presence.

Welcome to the magnificent world of the Law of Attraction. I am certain that you are flying over the moon already in anticipation of what is about to happen. Believe me, reality will only make you happier. Stay blessed, stay positive, and enjoy life!

REFERENCES

Anthony, K. (2017, December). *EFT Tapping*. Healthline; Healthline Media. https://www.healthline.com/health/eft-tapping

Cartwright, M. (2018, May 16). *Yin and Yang*. Ancient History Encyclopedia; Ancient History Encyclopedia. https://www.ancient.eu/Yin_and_Yang/

congerdesign. (2018). Heart Red Rope. In *Pixabay*. https://pixabay.com/photos/heart-red-rope-loyalty-love-3085515/

Deepak Chopra. (1994). *The seven spiritual laws of success: a practical guide to the fulfillment of your dreams*. Amber-Allen Pub.

Dieter44. (2018). Gem Citrine Stone Jewel Crystal. In *Pixabay*. https://pixabay.com/photos/gem-citrine-stone-jewel-crystal-3569938/

Emma Claire Donovan. (2019, January 16). *The Benefits of TRE for Stress, Anxiety, and Trauma*. Emma Donovan. https://emmaclairedonovan.com/2019/01/16/the-benefits-of-tre-for-stress-anxiety-and-trauma/

Free-Photos. (2014). Tea Cup Rest Afternoon. In *Pixabay*. https://pixabay.com/photos/tea-cup-rest-calm-afternoon-381235/

Free_Photos. (2015). Girl Blonde Sitting. In *Pixabay*. https://pixabay.com/photos/girl-blonde-sitting-lakeside-water-984065/

Gollwitzer, P. M., & Sheeran, P. (2006, January 1). *Implementation Intentions and Goal Achievement: A Meta-analysis of Effects and Processes*.

ScienceDirect; Academic Press. https://www.sciencedirect.com/science/article/pii/S0065260106380021

Good Interactive. (2014). Woman Person Sunset. In *Pixabay*. https://pixabay.com/photos/woman-person-sunset-dreams-alone-491623/

JacksonDavid. (2020). Woman Inspiration Dance. In *Pixabay*. https://pixabay.com/photos/woman-inspiration-dance-model-4775733/

Jaffe, E. (2011). Mirror Neurons: How We Reflect on Behavior. *APS Observer*, *20*(5). https://www.psychologicalscience.org/observer/mirror-neurons-how-we-reflect-on-behavior

Jung, J. Y., Oh, Y. H., Oh, K. S., Suh, D. W., Shin, Y. C., & Kim, H. J. (2007). Positive-Thinking and Life Satisfaction amongst Koreans. *Yonsei Medical Journal*, *48*(3), 371. https://doi.org/10.3349/ymj.2007.48.3.371

Justasurferdude. (2017). Rose Flower Wiltered. In *Pixabay*. https://pixabay.com/photos/rose-flower-wilted-floral-plant-2335203/

kalyanayahaluwo. (2020). Meditate Meditation Woman Mountains. In *Pixabay*. https://pixabay.com/photos/meditate-meditation-woman-mountains-5375835/

ktphotography. (2017). Candles Bright Light. In *Pixabay*. https://pixabay.com/photos/candles-bright-light-flame-2550688/

Marlene, C. (2018, July 29). *Ithaka: Journey not Destination*. Cheryl Marlene. https://www.cherylmarlene.com/ithaka-journey-not-destination/

Myriams-Fotos. (2017). Woman Beauty Rock. In *Pixabay*. https://pixabay.com/photos/woman-beauty-rock-sea-clouds-2724966/

petig. (2020). Sunset Woman Freedom. In *Pixabay*. https://pixabay.com/photos/sunset-woman-freedom-silhouette-5238044/

Pexels. (2016). Meditate Meditation Peaceful. In *Pixabay*. https://pixabay.com/photos/meditate-meditation-peaceful-1851165/

PIRO4D. (2016). Feng Shui Zen Stones. In *Pixabay*. https://pixabay.com/photos/feng-shui-zen-stones-texture-1927590/

Pitkanen, M. (2018, June). *(PDF) The experiments of Masaru Emoto with emotional imprinting of water*. ResearchGate. https://www.researchgate.net/publication/335909571_The_experiments_of_Masaru_Emoto_with_emotional_imprinting_of_water qimono. (2018). Drop Splash Drip. In *Pixabay*. https://pixabay.com/photos/drop-splash-drip-water-liquid-wet-3698073/

Smith, J. (2018, February 14). *The Emotional Vibration Analysis Frequency Chart*. Blisspot. https://blisspot.com/blogs/5719/654/the-emotional-vibration-analysis-frequency-chart

stokpic. (2015). Woman Working Bed. In *Pixabay*. https://pixabay.com/photos/woman-working-bed-laptop-typing-731894/

Valiphotos. (2015). Road Forest Season. In *Pixabay*. https://pixabay.com/photos/road-forest-season-autumn-fall-1072823/

Wikipedia Contributors. (2019, September 27). *All You Need Is Love*. Wikipedia; Wikimedia Foundation. https://en.wikipedia.org/wiki/All_You_Need_Is_Love

PLEASE LEAVE A REVIEW ON AMAZON

From the bottom of my heart, thank you for reading my book. I truly hope that it helps you on your spiritual journey and to live a more empowered and happy life. Would you be kind enough to leave an honest review for this book on Amazon? I would be ecstatic to read your feedback and it could impact the lives of others across the globe, giving them hope and power. I read **every** review I receive and each one helps me become the best writer I can be.

Thank you and good luck,

Angela Grace

JOIN OUR COMMUNITY

Why not join our Facebook community and discuss your spiritual path with like-minded seekers?

We would love to hear from you!

Go here to join the Ascending Vibrations community: **bit.ly/ascendingvibrations**

CLAIM YOUR FREE
AUDIOBOOK

DOWNLOAD THE *'SPIRITUAL CLEANSING'* AUDIOBOOK
INSTANTLY FOR FREE

If you love listening to audio books on-the-go, I have great news for you. You can download the audiobook version of *'Spiritual Cleansing'* for **FREE** just by signing up for a **FREE** 30-day audible trial! Turn the page for more details!

Audible trial benefits

As an audible customer, you'll receive the below benefits with you 30-day free trial:

• Free audible copy of this book

• After the trial, you will get 1 credit each month to use on any audiobook

• Your credits automatically roll over to the next month if you don't use them

• Choose from over 400,000 titles

• Listen anywhere with the audible app across multiple devices

• Make easy, no hassle exchanges of any audiobook you don't love

• Keep your audiobooks forever, even if you cancel your membership

• And much more

Click the links below to get started:

Go here for audible US:

bit.ly/spiritualcleansinglisten

Go here for audible UK:

bit.ly/spiritualcleansinglistenuk

Printed in the USA
CPSIA information can be obtained
at www.ICGtesting.com
LVHW080056091123
763364LV00005B/77